"When it comes to a topic as personal and private as one's body image, it takes an author with tremendous courage and willingness to be vulnerable to touch the hearts of readers. Amanda Martinez Beck is that author, and her book *Lovely: How I Learned to Embrace the Body God Gave Me* is surely that book, ready to touch the hearts of its readers. Packed with important truths from Scripture and Church teaching, moments of deep and powerful reflection, and a personal story that will relate to so many, this book is ready to touch hearts and reframe all of our thinking about the gift God has given us in our unique and beautifully created bodies."

— TOMMY TIGHE, author of *The Catholic Hipster Handbook* and co-host of *Repent & Submit* on CatholicTV

"I have witnessed too many homilies filled with body disparagement and calls to diet to lead a more holy life. For decades I have longed for the Church to have access to non-diet ways to relate to food, yet the diet industry and weight bias have kept it from us. Finally, I have a book that describes the dangerous distraction to diet along with futile focus on weight through the lens of Catholic teachings. Thank you, Amanda, for writing this book and sharing your story! I found it easy to read and deeply inspiring. I hope every member of the Catholic Church connects with her book's wisdom. Especially, I hope priests read it before they deliver homilies referring to food and bodies. This book helps us understand the important nuances of how we relate to food and how it can enhance or hinder our relationship with God and loving our neighbor."

— JULIE DUFFY DILLON, registered dietician and host of the *Love, Food* podcast

"Amanda Martinez Beck has written a lovely book that teaches women about loving their bodies the way they are and realizing that their bodies are perfect in the eyes of

God even when the world is telling them that they are imperfect. She intersperses her work with moving vignettes from her own journey from an insecure, overweight child to a confident size-dignity activist, and provides insightful questions for reflection as well as guidance in accepting one's body — and by extension, one's self — as a valuable gift with inherent worth and dignity in the eyes of God. This book is a must-read for any woman who has ever looked in the mirror and wished she had a different body."

— JoAnna Wahlund, *The Catholic Working Mother* (blog)

"In *Lovely*, Amanda Beck bypasses the trite statements we think we're supposed to make about our bodies and delves right into the tough questions about how we should view ourselves, body and soul, in light of the Gospel. A challenging, beautiful read!"

— Haley Stewart, blogger, podcaster, and author of *The Grace of Enough: Pursuing Less and Living More in a Throwaway Culture*

"When I was twelve, a stranger told me I had thick thighs, and 17 years later, I still think about that comment as examine my body in the mirror. *Lovely* is the first book I've read that asked to engage my whole person — mind, soul, body, and thick thighs — and I'm so glad I said yes. Achingly raw and vulnerable at points, this book never demands more than it gives as Amanda weaves together biblical insight, expert voices, and her own personal experiences. In bravely entering into this conversation, Amanda offers us a gift: a chance to dialogue with her on questions we've been too afraid to ask. I, for one, am so grateful for the chance to finally speak."

— Joy Beth Smith, author of *Party of One*

"There are so many plus-size models, so many plus-size retailers, so many people advocating for body love and body grace and body mercy in the world. But you'll only find those voices 'in the world.' What about those people who are in the world but not of the world? The fact of the matter is that when we go to church, when we are among the body of Christ, those voices are painfully absent, and, ironically, those of us with 'unconventional' bodies are often met with shame, scorn, derision and judgment as opposed to the peace, love, grace, and mercy the Church should be known for. Lovely advocates for body compassion and challenges us to see ourselves the way God sees us. 'My body tells my story' and 'Jesus loves my body.' Whew. It's a radical, almost revolutionary idea that ought not to be so radical: the idea that Jesus loves us as we are, *with* our bodies, *in* our bodies, our bodies *themselves*, and that he actually might be responsible for the story written in and by our bodies. Amanda reminds us that our bodies are instruments — not ornaments — to do the Lord's bidding. They are vehicles of his grace and kindness in this world. It may not be perfect, but it is good and holy, and God created it, so I shall learn to love it. I thank God for this book and I thank God for you, Amanda!"

— SIMONE SAMUELS, plus-sized fitness professional,
blogger, and Youtuber/host of *Sipping with Simone*,
www.Simonesamuels.ca

"Amanda Martinez Beck has written a book that is radical — that is, it gets to the root of so much of what ails our society. Her call to see ourselves as made for relationship with God, and to see our bodies as good no matter what, is holy work. This book beats back the forces of evil which long to ensnare and entrap and abuse, and replaces fear and self-hatred with love. Read it for yourselves, your families, and your neighbors. May we all learn to give grace to ourselves, that we might be able to give grace to our neighbors."

— D. L. MAYFIELD, activist and author of *Assimilate or Go Home:*
Notes from a Failed Missionary on Rediscovering Faith

"If you've ever experienced shame and frustration in regard to your physical self, Amanda Martinez Beck has words of mercy and grace you need to hear. In *Lovely: How I Learned to Embrace the Body God Gave Me*, Amanda challenges our commonly held notions of health and wellness for our greatest good. Through vivid personal stories and powerful biblical teaching, Amanda's gentle voice dislodges the various ways body shame has taken hold in our own hearts and lives. Readers of *Lovely* will learn how to extend mercy to the body God has given them, thereby becoming beacons of God's mercy to everyone they encounter — something we need more of in today's world."

— ERIN STRAZA, author of *Comfort Detox: Finding Freedom from Habits That Bind You*, co-host of *Persuasion Podcast*, and managing editor of *Christ and Pop Culture*

"In *Lovely: How I Learned to Embrace the Body God Gave Me*, Amanda Martinez Beck invites us to see our bodies the way the Creator made them, as good and lovely. In a world that constantly tells us how to fix our imperfect bodies, Amanda calls us into a better way. She asks us to see our bodies and the bodies of those around us as good, while acknowledging their weaknesses and flaws and pain. With personal stories and truths rooted in Scripture and Christian theology, Beck offers us a theology of the body that honors each body as made in the image of God. Beck's book is important reading for anyone who struggles to embrace their body and live fully into who God has created us to be."

— J. NICOLE MORGAN, author of *Fat and Faithful: Learning to Love Our Bodies, Our Neighbors, and Ourselves lovely*

lovely

How I Learned to Embrace the
Body God Gave Me

Amanda Martinez Beck

**Our
Sunday
Visitor**

www.osv.com
Our Sunday Visitor Publishing Division
Our Sunday Visitor, Inc.
Huntington, Indiana 46750

This book is dedicated to:

Zachary, *mi media naranja,* for his love and support

Saint John, for helping me to write so that my joy may
be complete

Saint Lawrence, for teaching me that I am the treasure
of the Church

Mary, for always carrying me to Jesus

Loving God,
pour into our hearts and lives
your healing Spirit,
that the sacredness of every human person
might be respected and protected
as the precious image of God.

Contents

Chapter 1

Siren Song

"But true love is the burden
that will carry me back
home
Carry me with the
memories of the beauty I
have known"

JOSH GARRELS, "ULYSSES"

Have you heard the story of Hannah from the Bible? With a love triangle, a little bit of religion, and a rivalry between two wives of the same man, it has all the hallmarks of a good soap opera. Hannah is the favorite wife of a man named Elkanah, but here's the rub: Elkanah's other wife, Peninah, has all the babies. Hannah's body is unable to give her what she desperately craves: a baby of her own. The failure of her body to bear children fills her with pain and lament.

Elkanah begs Hannah to see that her body's limitations don't diminish his love for her. He says, "Hannah, why do you weep? And why do you not eat? And why is your heart sad? Am I not more to you than ten sons?" (1 Sam 1:8). She ignores him and goes off by herself to bargain with God for what she wants, so loudly that the priest Eli thinks she is drunk. He tells her she is making a fool of herself and that she needs to sober up, but she responds: "No, my lord, I am a woman sorely troubled; I have drunk neither wine nor strong drink, but I have been pouring out my soul before the LORD. Do not regard your maidservant as a base woman, for all along I have been speaking out of my great anxiety and vexation" (1 Sam 1:15–16).

The first time I read Hannah's story, I was sixteen years old, and I felt Hannah's pain. Except it wasn't a baby I was longing for. It was a different body. I don't mean to minimize the pain of infertility; indeed, Hannah's pain at her inability to conceive would be reality for me almost ten years later. But my life at that point was marked by two distinct things: first, my desire to seek God above all else, and second, to have a smaller, thinner body so that I could be happy and enjoy my life and be all that God made me to be.

Even as a sixteen-year-old, in Elkanah's tender plea, I sensed God speaking to me.

"Amanda, why do you weep? And why is your heart grieved? Am I not better to you than ten size-4 dresses?"

"Yes, Lord, you are," I responded, even though my heart's song of longing still played on in its minor key. I committed to seeking first God's kingdom, hoping all things being added unto me would include a new, slimmer body. But even as I did my best to heed the prophet Micah's words to do justice, to love mercy, and to walk humbly with God, my body stayed fat. It not only stayed fat, it got fatter.

In a culture that proclaims a gospel of thinness as salvation, I was clearly headed to hell in a handbasket full of fattening processed food.

If I were writing a memoir about my body, I'd subvert the before-and-after picture trope. Both pictures are of a fat Amanda, but the before picture is a girl who wanted a different body and who thought negatively about herself all the time, all while trying to love God and love her neighbor as herself. The after picture is a snapshot of her as happy as she has learned to be, knowing she is fat *and* loved by God, loving him back and enjoying her neighbors. Somewhere in between the before and after shots, I learned that if I were in a different body than the one God gave me, I wouldn't be me anymore.

I didn't set out to become an activist. I am a fat woman who writes a lot and isn't afraid to speak the truth and call out inconsistency when I see it. I certainly never thought I'd be writing a book about faith and fatness. I just found myself writing and speaking out more about bodies and Christianity. The more I wrote, the more I heard from other people about their experiences, and the more I realized that people of girth need to know their worth in the eyes of God. There is so much that the teachings of the Catholic Church have to offer us, so much that can help us live happy lives in our good bodies, no matter what size we are.

When you use the word "fat," people start to get uncomfortable. I understand it; we have attached a morality to fatness that gets defenses up. I have often encountered well-meaning people who think fat acceptance is a celebration of gluttony. It is not. It is, instead, a celebration of the dignity of the human person — a dignity that isn't dependent on clothing size or the number on the scale.

Then this question inevitably comes up: "So, what about health?" Yes, health is important. I do want to acknowledge, though, that as beautifully complex beings, there's a lot more to talk about than just physical health. A major motivation behind this book is to help us retrain ourselves to think about health more holistically and to consider our bodies in terms of mercy, kindness, and wonder, rather than criticism, failure, and self-loathing.

It's hard to have a conversation about bodies without talking about physical health specifically (which we will do in this book), but for now, suffice it to say that I see health as a balance of four aspects of the human being: the physical, the mental, the spiritual, and the emotional. I like to think of these four components of health as the wheels on a 4x4. If one is out of whack, it cannot fulfill its purpose. Each wheel must be calibrated and fully functioning to engage in its intended task. Our culture focuses on physical health, so that "tire" gets all the air and care. So it's no surprise that our society tends to get stuck in muddy places.

> A major motivation behind this book is to help us retrain ourselves to think about health more holistically and to consider our bodies in terms of mercy, kindness, and wonder, rather than criticism, failure, and self-loathing.

The simple truth is that every person, no matter their size, is valuable in the Kingdom of God. This truth has spurred me on to write this book. Our society has constructed a moral system around fatness and the implied superiority of thinness, where fat bodies are bad and thin bodies are good, no questions asked. Sadly, this has crept into our Church as well. This book will talk openly about the purpose of bodies, what makes a body good, and the need to reframe the way we think and speak about our bodies and the bodies of the people around us.

The sirens of our culture wail persistently, and their call to thinness is loud and persuasive. They sing to us that in appearance and fitness are the foundations of personal worthiness. The siren song of thinness can be intoxicating, and like strong drink it affects our minds and our bodies. We constantly hear the message of becoming our "true selves" through weight loss and dieting. We are inundated with images of happy thinness and attractive athleticism, a gospel of freedom from fat and loneliness that feeds on our insecurities.

Yet we must proclaim and live the truth. God loves each of us as we are, and he invites us to join in the beauty of the Church's song. My body is good and valuable, as all bodies are. I want to challenge you to bind yourself to this truth, and to begin to think about bodies, faith, and fatness in a fresh way, so that you can counter the siren song of our broken world with a healing song of your own.

For reflection

What aspects of my body do I bring before the Lord in frustration, like Hannah did? What do I think God is asking me in response?

Do I believe that I'm valuable in the kingdom of God? What beliefs, fears, or insecurities are holding me back from believing this?

Chapter 2

Mercy

> *"It takes enormous trust and courage to allow yourself to remember."*

BESSEL A. VAN DER KOLK

"Jesus Christ is the face of the Father's mercy." These words opened Pope Francis's declaration of the Year of Mercy, which began on the Feast of the Immaculate Conception in 2015. Every diocese in the world opened its Door of Mercy for pilgrims to come and encounter God-made-flesh. I was a relatively new Catholic, and this was my first Jubilee year. I was excited to be a pilgrim myself, journeying to the doors of my diocesan cathedral to receive the mercy promised to me.

During this Jubilee year, the Church urged us in a special way to receive mercy from God and his Church for ourselves so that we can extend it to others. The Holy Father wrote, "At times we are called to gaze even more attentively on mercy so that we may become a more effective sign of the Father's action in our lives." And when it came to offering mercy, I had room to grow. I could offer it more to my children and husband on a daily basis. But the person in my life who needed my mercy most, especially when it came to my body, was me.

> My body tells my story.

In that Jubilee year, I found myself a pilgrim, praying before the Blessed Sacrament in a chapel far from home. I looked up at the cross above the tabernacle, with the image of a broken man in agony, suspended between heaven and earth. In front of me was the monstrance, the crafted metal display stand for the consecrated host, Christ in the flesh.

My body tells my story.

The words pressed themselves against my heart, and I considered them. The story in front of me — on the crucifix and in the monstrance — was told in nails and wood, blood and sweat, in a body broken for me, to eat and to remember. It is a story I love, this story that the body of Jesus tells.

I looked down at my own body. Could it really tell

my story? I sighed, because this question scared me. I was not sure I wanted to know what story my body was telling. There was so much about my body that I wanted to change. So much that I wanted to cover up. So much that I hated. I wished I could hide it most of the time. My body made me feel so vulnerable, and that made me angry. But Pope Francis was calling me to mercy, not just to others but to myself, and that had to include my body. I knew I had to choose whether I would engage the story before me, and it was a hard — and scary — choice to make. It was scary, first of all, because it meant that I had to remember.

I remember becoming aware of my body and how it didn't exactly fit anywhere. I remember me in my favorite red sweater, and the taunts from boys on the playground in their newly acquired Spanish vocabulary. They called me *grande rojo* — "big red." Even more, I remember the mix of emotions their nickname gave me; yes, they were being cruel, but they were giving me attention that I craved.

I remember sitting at the piano as a preteen with messy hair and no fashion sense whatsoever, my piano teacher giving me advice on losing weight so that the dimple in my chin would go away. I fumbled with the keys while the sting of her words pushed me deeper into hating my body as it displayed my weakness and failings.

I reach further back to pull out one of the earliest memories I have of my body, in a closet with two neighbor boys my age. We are hiding from the light so they can touch me to satisfy their curiosity, and so I can earn the kiss I've wanted from them. My cheeks flush as I remember the closet door thrown open, one of their mothers finding us, seeing what was happening, and never speaking of it again.

More memories swirl around in my psyche, and I realize that every memory I have that is connected to my body is full of shame, regret, guilt, and hatred. Is that true for you, too?

The mercy of remembering

It's hard work, diving in and remembering. So many memories we have are painful, and it's normal to avoid things that hurt us or make us uncomfortable. If memories of our bodies bring up shame or hatred, more than likely we will avoid those memories. Here's the problem, though: if you avoid the pain and shame, neglecting the work of going through tough memories, they don't just disappear. I am who I am today because of all the experiences I have had. If I choose to ignore or avoid the hard ones, I don't fully know or understand myself. If I just stuff them or hide them away? That will never lead to lasting peace. This is true for all of us.

If memories are not addressed intentionally, they will continue to interfere with our normal operating systems. In *The Body Keeps the Score: Brain, Mind, and Body in the Healing of Trauma*, Bessel A. van der Kolk writes:

> We may think we can control our grief, our terror, or our shame by remaining silent, but naming offers the possibility of a different kind of control. When Adam was put in charge of the animal kingdom in the Book of Genesis, his first act was to give a name to every living creature. If you've been hurt, you need to acknowledge and name what happened to you.... Feeling listened to and understood changes our physiology; being able to articulate a complex feeling, and having our feelings recognized, lights up our limbic brain and creates an "aha" moment. (232)

Though Dr. van der Kolk is writing specifically for

people who have post-traumatic stress disorder — where sufferers have endured violence, neglect, or abuse — we can draw from his wisdom. When we feel shame arise, we need to investigate why we feel that way. This is because when we can remember where that seed of shame was planted, we can go back to up-root it. That is an act of mercy toward ourselves.

> When we can remember where that seed of shame was planted, we can go back to uproot it. That is an act of mercy toward ourselves.

For example, when I look in the mirror, I am tempted to be very critical of my knock knees. Not only do they prevent me from standing with my feet to-gether, but as much as I scrub them, the skin covering my knees is darker than the rest of my (very white) legs. Feelings of shame arise, and I am tempted to hate my whole body.

Yet I believe that every body is a good body, without question, even bodies with knock knees. So why do I have shame about my knees? It's not because they don't work well — they do. It's not because I judge other peo-ple for their knees — I don't. But when I was a child, someone I loved made a comment. They told me how distinct my knees were, and that if I exercised a certain way, they might stop knocking together. I was ashamed *because someone told me that I should be.* It's a painful mem-ory, because I was so young, and I internalized the com-ment as a rejection of my body and therefore of me, too.

The mercy of God, though, enables me to go back to these memories and see the truth about my experience. In his mercy, I can see myself as the little girl I was then. I can see the person looking at my body critically, and I can see the self-hatred of their own body that they unconsciously expressed in the words they said to me. I can recognize that while I internalized their comment as a rejection of my body and of myself, it was not really that. Bringing that memory into the light of God's mercy, as hard and as painful as that can be, allows me to see the truth that sets me free. My knees are not bad just because someone else thought they were, and I am under no obligation to hate them. There is no shame in having discolored knock knees. They are my knees, and they do amazing things!

Just because I have remembered that moment of shame regarding my knees, however, doesn't mean that I don't still struggle with judging my body. The difference is, now that I have named that experience and called out the lie that says knock knees are shameful, I can counter the tape player in my head that gets on to me about my knees. Over time, the volume of that tape player gets turned down and down and down, until I can't even hear it anymore.

Wearing shorts — something I used to approach with apprehension — is now an act of defiance I perform against the commentary that my knees are somehow not good. Naming the shame has given me power over it, and I can press on in loving God and loving my neighbor as myself, even with knock knees. If we fail to embrace the stories that our bodies are telling, if we don't name our painful memories and thereby release ourselves from their power, we can't fully engage in the world around us. Dr. van der Kolk writes, "As long as you keep secrets and suppress information, you are fundamentally at war with yourself. Hiding your core feelings takes an enormous amount of energy, it saps your motivation to pursue worthwhile goals, and it leaves you feeling bored and shut down" (232).

Practically, what does it look like to do the hard work of remembering? First, you have to pay attention to your feelings. When feelings of shame or regret come up, follow them back through your life — where have you felt like this before? Is there an experience connected with this shame? As you begin to map out the memories, ask God to help you see yourself through his eyes of mercy. Recognize any lies you believed about yourself because of what happened and uproot the seeds of shame that were sown. By removing the seeds of shame and instead sowing seeds of mercy in those memories of the past, you are preparing yourself to reap a harvest of mercy for your body today. And when you start to live out the story your body is telling with mercy and joy, others will be drawn into it. As my friend Nicole Morgan writes in her book *Fat and Faithful*, "Courage begets courage."

Remember with Mary

Fortunately, we are not alone on this journey. One of my favorite things to do is to spend time before the Blessed Sacrament when I need help getting my heart and mind on the same track.

Before the monstrance that contains the consecrated host, we can start the hard work of remembering, trusting Jesus to carry us. We can let ourselves be drawn into Christ's story. I place myself there, at the foot of Jesus' cross during the crucifixion. Jesus hangs above me, looking at me with love mixed with pain, and he speaks to me: "Amanda, behold your mother." I look to the side, to where his eyes are pointing me, and suddenly I am a child, weeping and longing for comfort. Mary takes me up into her lap, and as we sit at the foot of the cross together, she starts to teach me.

Like a child does, I grab at a string of beads around her neck. She reaches up and pulls the strand over her head and puts the beads in my hand. "This is how I've learned to treasure these things in my heart," she whispers in my ear, and she begins to tell me about the mysteries that she has experienced — joyful ones, luminous ones, and right now, sorrowful ones. "The glorious ones are yet to come," she tells me. The sadness in her voice is tinged with the smallest bit of hope, as we sit together beneath the crucified Jesus.

The Rosary can serve each of us as a guide as we sift through out own memories of our bodes. Yes, the reason that we pray the Rosary is to gain understanding of the life of Jesus through Mary's eyes, to journey with her from the Annunciation all the way to her crowning. And as I journey through these memories with Mary and learn to meet God in these mysteries of the Most Holy Rosary, I also learn that I can meet him in my own set of memories, too.

What memories would be on your set of beads? If our bodies tell our stories, then that means we have to confront our memories so we can learn that story and learn to see that it is good and beautiful. For myself, this means I have to pull up many memories that are painful — excruciating, even. I don't know if I am brave enough to do the hard work of remembering.

> The Rosary can serve each of us as a guide as we sift through our own memories of our bodies.

That's where Mary comes to help me. And I am confident that she will come to help you, too. She urges each of us to take up our beads and map out our stories — all the mysteries that we have seen and experienced in our bodies. The joyful ones, the luminous ones, and even the sorrowful ones. "The glorious ones are coming," she promises. Her promise gives us courage to remember. The sorrow and pain point us toward glory on this journey with God, and that knowledge can give us strength to do the hard work of remembering.

Look at the crucifix. See the broken and bleeding form of the Son of God. His body was broken for you and for me. Even in his brokenness and pain, the body of Jesus is good. This broken God-man lets his body tell us his story, and with tenderness and gentleness he invites us to embrace our own body's weakness. He invites each of us to see the story that our body is telling, leading us to the place where we can truly say: "My body is good, and I love the story that it tells."

Let Jesus come with you as you begin the work of re-membering. Let him lay his hands on your memories. This is the mercy of Jesus — he may not erase the pain, but at his touch your sadness can comingle with joy. Your memories are like the mysteries of Mary's Rosary, distinct points in your life that lead you to the cross, to the resurrection, and to the glory of a deep and abiding relationship with God.

It is my hope that you will feel brave enough to look at your own story-telling body with joy instead of loathing. Maybe you just can't believe that your body is good, right now, right where you find yourself. I hope that changes as you read this book. Thank you for joining me on this jour-ney, and believe me when I say that it is a journey worth taking.

For reflection

Who in my life needs my mercy?

What story do I think my body has to tell?

What memories of my body can I bring before the Lord, with Mary's help?

What are the sorrowful, painful mysteries I need to allow Jesus to touch so he can heal them?

Chapter 3

This Is My Body

"You are enough.
You are not too much."

J. NICOLE MORGAN

I found an old keychain when my parents moved out of the house where I grew up. The keychain is shaped like a megaphone, and if you hold the smaller end up to your eye, you can see an image against the cap on the larger end. The keychain itself is only about two inches long, and its pink-and-white body is etched with golden letters, the name and number of a long-forgotten Little League photographer.

The picture inside is of me at age five, at bat for my tee-ball team. The sun catches the curls of my very long, very dark hair cascading over my hot pink jersey. Emblazoned on my shirt in bold white font is our team name: "The Flamingos" (or "The Flaming O's" as I liked to think of it, playing with words even before I could read chapter books). My right elbow is cocked, ready to swing. My batting form is pretty good for a kindergartner, but while I wish I could smile with affection for kid-me, all I can see is my belly making itself seen and my knees that knock together. It's always been like this, my body — and I hated it.

Growing up in Southern evangelical culture, it was impressed upon me from a young age that a good and holy woman should be three things: small, gentle, and quiet. As a large, outspoken, and passionate person on the verge of womanhood, I had three strikes against me. I have always been too big, with a big frame, big feet, a big personality, big feelings, big dreams, and a big voice. My bigness just kept bumping into others' expectations and demands, and for many years I nursed the resulting bruises in loneliness.

Over time, I found that I could cover up the "too big" parts of my personality. It was harder to cover up the bigness of my body, but I tried to do that as well. By the time I reached seventh grade, I knew two things: I knew that I was smart, and I knew that I was fat. I didn't have to hide the smart part. It earned me social capital and affection and praise from the adults in my life, and in the magnet program I was surrounded by other bright kids. Somehow, though, I was the biggest girl in my grade, despite having been on restrictive diets for as long as I could remember.

I made sure that I had a sweater with me at all times, even though it was sweltering East Texas, where you only actually need a sweater twelve days out of the year. I carried it with me because I needed something to cover up all my fat rolls. The desks in my language arts classroom were the typical American style: a blue plastic chair to slide into from the side, where your predominant writing arm would be supported by a composite wood writing surface that spread from your side to the front of your midsection. I can still hear the twang of the metal basket on the desk in front of me as my feet found a place to perch. My right arm was tucked in, cradled nicely against the right side of the desk chair and armrest, but my left side was completely exposed. My belly could not escape notice, so I brought a sweater every day to cover up my disgusting fat rolls and to protect myself from others' stares and comments. Have you ever tried to cover your body because you were ashamed?

> Have you ever tried to cover your body because you were ashamed?

My weight didn't fluctuate up and down; it steadily climbed, and it was always the thing I despised most about myself. Not uncommon, right? Throughout high school and college, my weight defined me and I always felt on the outskirts of "normal." Imagine my relief when in grad school I met a man who fell madly in love with me — fat body and all! And imagine my shame, after we were engaged and then even more so after we were married, as my weight continued to climb.

In July 2011, I sat in a doctor's office after an overnight sleep study, hoping to get help for a possible diagnosis of sleep apnea. It's a serious condition for several reasons, including oxygen deprivation to your brain and the inability to stay in a REM cycle to get the restorative rest that only comes from deep sleep. I knew something was wrong. I couldn't make it through a day of teaching Spanish at my university without a siesta during my lunch break. I had no energy to do anything after work, so I became isolated from my community. I got shingles from the stress of my seemingly low-stress life — no kids, a great spouse, a job I loved and at which I excelled, and a dream housing situation on campus, hanging out with college students. I hadn't slept well in months (at least), and I was in this appointment, desperate for help.

Going to the doctor is a vulnerable thing to do, and having someone there in solidarity can be reassuring. So, for my initial consult with the doctor, my husband tagged along. During that first visit, while Dr. Barrels* had not been warm, exactly, we learned that he was Catholic. That was exciting for my husband and me, because although we were still Protestants, we found ourselves increasingly drawn to the truth and beauty expressed in the Catholic Church. Turning to the issue at hand, Dr. Barrels spoke with us about the correlation between weight gain and sleep apnea, but he mentioned that there is some debate about which causes the other. This was encouraging, because I had put on a bit of weight since our marriage. My husband and I left that appointment encouraged that we would get some answers, and it felt like we had a connection at some level with this doctor.

When I went back for the results of my sleep study, I felt confident enough to go into the appointment by myself and told my husband that he could read his book in the lobby and wait for me to finish. When I was called back, I sat in the exam room alone for a few minutes. There was a knock at the door and the doctor came in and sat on a stool across from me. We exchanged pleasantries, and then he looked me in the eye.

"So, when did you get fat?"

His words were cold. His eyes were fixed on mine as he waited for me to answer. I was taken aback. I am usually

---

* Not his real name.

one to give the benefit of the doubt, however, so I overcame my surprise and explained that yes, I had gained a specific number of pounds since meeting and marrying my husband two years before.

"And your weight before that?"

After I told him, he responded, "That was still fat." I sat there in quiet disbelief. The f-word fell from his lips with such ease! Dr. Barrels went on to discuss the results of my sleep study. At least, I think that's what he talked about. My only memories from that part of our conversation are of my face flushing in embarrassment, debating while I sat there whether I would mention this interchange to my husband. It's not that I wasn't used to this particular f-word, nor was I unaware that the number on the scale had implications for my body and my place in society. Mostly, my shock came from his candor that crossed the line into rudeness and cruelty. Even though most Americans believe that being fat is an exclusively negative thing, most people I had interacted with to that point — whether doctors or laypeople — used softened terms like "overweight" or the medically relevant "obese."

The way this doctor spoke to me was malicious, an attempt to put my fat body in its shameful place. The encounter shook me deeply. Apparently, in Dr. Barrels's eyes, I did not deserve to be treated with kindness or dignity. My body in its fat condition — and who knows how many hundreds of fat people he treated — was wrong and shameful and deserving of guilt and ridicule. From that moment, my anxiety about going to the doctor increased significantly. If someone in a position of cultural and intellectual authority like a doctor could speak to me like this and make me feel worthless, did that mean I actually deserved it?

The encounter with Dr. Barrels left me feeling like my voice was taken away. In my mind, it stood to reason that if someone tasked with caring for me could treat me like this, others could, too. And not only doctors — also pastors, bosses, and even those I called friends. Dr. Barrels accused me of being fat as if it were a moral failure for which I needed to repent. Because of how my body looked and how much it weighed, I was guilty, unworthy, too much, and simultaneously not enough. For too long, I believed in that doctor's version of me. And that belief boiled down to this statement: *I have nothing to offer God or other people because I am fat.*

Perhaps you look back at pictures of your childhood with disdain and self-loathing. Perhaps you're still sitting in the classroom chair trying to cover up your fat rolls. Or perhaps you've had an experience like mine with a doctor, where someone who was supposed to have your best interest in mind made it clear they thought you were not worthy. If any of these are true, don't be afraid to go back to these moments. Write them out. Be brave and remember. If you want to move forward in loving this good body God has given you, you have to go into the past and root out the lies you have believed.

> If you want to move forward in loving this good body God has given you, you have to go into the past and root out the lies you have believed.

See the tee-ball photo and love that little you. Put your hand on the shoulder of seventh-grade you and tell her that she doesn't have to separate her smarts and her body to be accepted. Go into that doctor's office and challenge the person in the position of cultural power (a doctor, a parent, or a thin friend) and defend the person in the vulnerable place. Like I've said before (and will likely say many times again), this is hard but it is worth the work. When you let the negative memories and feelings of your body come out of hiding and be dealt with in the light, their power is lessened.

Encountering the Blessed Sacrament

I love all of the sacraments and I am so refreshed when I participate in them. But there is one that nourishes me in a way that is almost too beautiful to put into words: the Eucharist. In this sacrament, we receive Jesus into our mouths, he comes into our bodies, and the molecules of his flesh and blood disperse themselves through our bodies and our digestive systems. What a humble thing for the God of the universe to do! He makes himself accessible on a daily basis to literally feed his sheep! Even as I type this out now, I can't get over how amazing this is. It is truly a thing to be thankful for, which is the literal meaning of the Greek word *eucharistia* — "thanksgiving, gratitude."

Jesus has a body, and it is broken for me. For you. He doesn't cringe when he sees images of himself in the past. He doesn't cover up his wounded hands, feet, and side when he communes with us. And, as the Great Physician, he certainly never comes at us with accusation or blame when we are in need of his help. He is completely confident in who he is in his body, so he doesn't have to play the power games that we are so often drawn into.

When we eat his flesh and drink his blood, we participate in his life (Jn 6). The flesh of Jesus is good. He comes and makes his home with each of us day after day, week after week, through the Eucharist. When I read Genesis 1 and 2, I can almost see God smile on the sixth day of creation, when he forms Adam from the dust and Eve from Adam's side. "One day, in these very good bodies," I imagine him saying, "my flesh will find a home — and what a good home it will be!" And when we consider that the God of the universe makes his home inside our very bodies, can we consider our own bodies as anything but good?

For reflection

What memories of my body still cause me pain or sorrow?

How have others made me feel unworthy and ashamed because of my body? Have I ever done that to others? What opportunities do I have to extend mercy as I have received it?

Do I allow Jesus in the Blessed Sacrament to say to me, "This is my body ... for you"? If not, why not?

Chapter 4

My Good Body

"Self-rejection is the greatest enemy of the spiritual life because it contradicts the sacred voice that calls us the 'Beloved.' Being the Beloved expresses the core truth of our existence."

HENRI NOUWEN

When it comes to my body, I have internalized so many expectations for it. The right size, the right weight, the right resting heart rate — all of these have been verbalized to me at some point in my life by people I care for. I can tell you this: trying to be perfect in multiple areas of your life so that you fulfill others' expectations of you is exhausting. As a people pleaser and a perfectionist, by the time I was a senior in college, I was in a bad place. My anxiety over failing at being perfect led me into a deep depression. I lay in bed a lot and I could barely make it to class. I was too afraid to get out of bed and encounter people, because I knew I would fail them. This even applied to people I would pass on the sidewalk on the way to class. It was a dark place.

Because it took so much energy just to get to and engage in class, I was very careful about the routes I chose to walk across campus. I valued efficiency more than anything, because I knew that if I spent too much of myself on the people around me, I might not be able to make it out of bed the next morning. One afternoon, I was walking home using the most efficient route, when I felt an overwhelming sense to slow down and take a more leisurely route to my apartment. This new path took me by a tree that I had seen before but never really noticed. On this day, though, I noticed it, because there were literally thousands of monarch butterflies resting on it and flapping their wings. To this day, it remains one of the most beautiful things I have ever seen. Standing there for a solid fifteen minutes, staring at these majestic insects who must have been migrating, I felt a spark of hope in my heart. I knew without doubt that God had led me to this tree, to share this experience with me. My goal had been efficiency for the sake of protecting myself, but his goal had been relationship with me, and always had been.

Efficiency had been my measure of perfection for myself; the more efficient I was, the better I felt about myself. My obsession with efficiency could also be seen in my attitude toward my body. How fast could I shower? What was the most efficient way to shave my legs and save time? I suppose I thought the less time I spent on my body, the better off I would be. I wouldn't be like *them* — the people who selfishly fretted over their bodies. That was so unspiritual and ungodly, right? If I couldn't be thin or athletic or whatever society told me I needed to be, at least I would be smart. I would be efficient. But I was actually hiding the sadness and disappointment I felt about my body behind a mask of intelligence and efficiency.

You can probably think of a time when the imperfections of your body were overwhelming. The right number on the scale could justify all the unhappiness you felt toward your body. The right number on the tag on your jeans could somehow make all the other issues you wanted to ignore fade into the background. Efficiency was something I focused on so that I didn't have to deal with the bigger issue of hating my body and its flaws. A significant shift happened for me, however, when I started to consider what the goal of my body is. Is the goal perfection? Efficiency? Flawlessness? Muscularity? Beauty? Smallness? Goodness?

The distinction between *perfect* and *good*

Have you ever read Matthew 5:48 and gotten a little bit uncomfortable? That's the part of the Sermon on the Mount where Jesus says, "You, therefore, must be perfect, as your heavenly Father is perfect." Don't you wish that Jesus had said, "Try to be perfect" instead? For many years, this command from Jesus gave me a lot of grief, partially because I had a pass/fail mentality when it came to how I was doing at anything. If I screwed up, I felt God must be mad at me because I had failed. That made me buckle down and work harder, only to fail again. It was a cycle of failure that led to self-loathing both of my body and my soul. I finally realized that I had to work on understanding what Jesus was actually saying in Matthew 5:48. My cultural understanding of "perfect" only made me feel like a hopeless failure, and that's not what Jesus wants for any of us.

In our culture, when we use the word "perfect" to describe something, we usually mean "flawless." The perfect face has no blemishes; the perfect belly has no love handles; the perfect skin has no wrinkles or stretch marks. According to this standard of flawlessness, the perfect body has no illness, no disability, and no inadequacy. Flawlessness, however, is a false notion of perfection.

> My cultural understanding of "perfect" only made me feel like a hopeless failure, and that's not what Jesus wants for any of us.

The word that is translated as "perfect" in Matthew 5:48 — *teleios* — doesn't mean "flawless." It means "brought to its end, finished; lacking nothing necessary to completeness, perfect; full grown." It is a form of the Greek word *telos*, which means "the end, the aim, the purpose." It stands to reason, then, that Jesus is calling us to be complete, to fulfill our purpose the way God the Father is complete and fulfills his purpose (which I am convinced is simply to be who he is, like he tells Moses at the burning bush in Exodus 3:14).

Do you think of your body in terms of perfection? What if you could step back and see your body through the lens of its purpose and its goal, rather than through the critical eye that demands flawlessness? One way I have been able to wrap my mind and heart around this, both for my body and my soul, is to meditate on the words of Saint Paul in Philippians 1:6: "And I am sure that he who began a good work in you will bring it to completion at the day of Christ Jesus." The Greek word for "completion" is *epiteleo*, which is related to *telos*. God will bring me — body and soul — to fulfill my purpose in his timing. And when

I can stop fretting over whether I'm doing things perfectly or not, I can start to understand that my body is good, even though it contains many things our culture perceives as flaws.

Healing hashtags

For all its detractors, the hashtag phenomenon of the millennial generation has borne fruit that is lasting. Who hasn't experienced what can only be expressed as #blessed? Of course, there is #yolo, our less erudite but more accessible *carpe diem*. On a more serious note, the hashtags #blacklivesmatter and #metoo have instigated awareness of the need for changes in our culture in how we treat each other, between races and sexes.

I came across #allbodiesaregoodbodies on Instagram as I was writing about my body, which happens to be, among other things, a fat body. The phrase struck at something in my heart, and I found myself using these precise words when talking with my children about bodies, and with my oldest daughter Lily, especially. I think a lot of things in my head, but once I speak them to my children, I want to know without a doubt that they are true and will produce good fruit in our lives.

I wrote several blog posts on the topic of all bodies being good, and I was surprised at the pushback I got. I didn't really think that saying all bodies are good bodies would be confrontational, but it was. One reader in particular, Mitch from Australia, took issue with my position. "I keep trying to reconcile how an unhealthy body can be a good body," he wrote. "I get that every body has goodness because every body has been created by God, and each person in his image. I keep likening it to an unkempt garden. Gardens take work and tending to flourish and I guess I see healthy as good — spiritually, emotionally, physically […] because Jesus came to heal the sick. I'm aware that healthy can look different for different body shapes, but I'm struggling to see how we can call an unhealthy body a good body — regardless of it being skinny or fat."

The real question here, I think, has to do with what is truly good about our bodies. In other words, we have to ask ourselves: Is health the goal for our body? If not, what is?

The prevailing culture tells me that a healthy body is the most important thing I can possess, and that health is the ultimate goal for my body. The cultural definition of healthy is more comprehensive than merely being free of illness; it

> We have to ask ourselves: Is health the goal for our body? If not, what is?

also includes the size and shape of a body. Men must be big and strong; women must be small and toned. Any body that does not fit within these specifications is not a good body.

Asking good questions

For me as a Catholic, I look to the teaching of the Church through Scripture and Tradition to help me understand what the goal of our bodies actually is. The *Catechism of the Catholic Church* is a big and beautiful work, containing the teachings of the Church distilled into specific points. It draws on Scripture, Church documents, and the writings of the saints. While I love how comprehensive it is, it can feel a little overwhelming. Thankfully, the Church has provided the *Compendium of the Catechism of the Catholic Church*, a short and sweet summary of the main points of Church teaching. It's my starting place when I'm thinking through tough questions regarding faith and life. I am really interested in stories — why we tell stories and how they move us. In fact, the narrative power of the *Catechism* is one more thread that God used to draw me into the Catholic Church. In any story, the first question that is being asked is "Who am I?" The second is "Do I matter?" The Church cannot, and in fact does not, shy away from these questions. Because I live in an incarnated reality — body and soul inseparable — I am asking these questions not only for my soul but for my body as well. It's convenient, then, that the *Catechism* and the *Compendium* are set up in a question-and-answer format! The following paragraph is the first question and answer found in the *Compendium*:

> What is the plan of God for man? God, infinitely perfect and blessed in himself, in a plan of sheer goodness freely created man to make him share in his own blessed life. In the fullness of time, God the Father sent his Son as the Redeemer and Savior of mankind, fallen into sin, thus calling all into his Church and, through the work of the Holy Spirit, making them adopted children and heirs of his eternal happiness. (1)

I want you to go back and read that paragraph out loud. What do you sense that second time through? For me, it's joy. Excitement for this "plan of sheer goodness" floods my soul, and my body responds, too. The hair on my arms stands up in anticipation. My heart gets strangely warm. Some people say that the purpose of humankind is "to glorify God," which is true, but that phrasing can seem really abstract for me. But when I hear that this is really a "plan of sheer goodness" for me to share in God's blessed existence? That I can dream about, wrap the fingers of my imagination around. That is life-changing for my body and my soul.

Everything in creation starts with the goodness, perfection, and blessing of God. Glory without goodness easily turns dictatorial, and we can start to think that the will of God is a tightrope rather than an open field (cf. Ps 18:20). It is only when we understand these truths about God that we can unpack what glory actually is and grasp how we, as human beings created in his image, can give him the glory he is due. Saint Irenaeus famously wrote that "the glory of God is man fully alive." Many of us have tried to limit ourselves, to be flawless, or to fit into a false ideal, but here is one of God's saints giving us permission to be fully alive. And to be fully alive must include our bodies and our souls, and not our souls alone. Seeking to understand what Irenaeus meant led me to realize that it's not just the soul that is made in God's image; the body is, too. And God created these bodies of ours as a part of his plan of sheer goodness. So how can I see my body in relation to God's plan of sheer goodness toward me?

> How can I see my body in relation to God's plan of sheer goodness toward me?

In his landmark work *Theology of the Body*, Pope John Paul II begins with an analysis of the text of Matthew 19:3–8. The Pharisees ask Jesus a question about marriage and divorce. Instead of giving a plain answer, he asks them a question in return, one that points them back to the beginning, to the Garden of Eden, where God established marriage between man and woman. Jesus wants the Pharisees to see the original purpose of marriage so they can see that the question they ask lacks a depth of understanding.

In a similar way, we need to turn our eyes and hearts back to the beginning to get at the original purpose of bodies. From the beginning, God created us in his image, and he looked at everything he made and found it very good. It's up to us to affirm the goodness of God's creation, especially in our own bodies.

What does it take for a body to be good? According to classical philosophy, a thing is good when it fulfills its purpose. A good sermon illuminates the Scripture, enabling us to swim in the truth of God and be washed by the water of the Word. That is the purpose of the sermon — to instruct and teach. A good school is one that prepares its students well to leave home and engage in society. That is the school's purpose — to prepare and train. What, then, is the purpose for a body? What allows us to say with confidence that all bodies are good bodies?

The *Catechism of the Catholic Church* helps us answer this question. The section of the *Catechism* on the creation of mankind helps us see God's purpose in creating us and how our bodies and souls form our complete selves. It's not merely our souls that are created in God's image, but our bodies, too. The *Catechism* says:

> "God created man in his own image" ... [and in man's] own nature he unites the spiritual and material worlds. (355)

> The human person, created in the image of God, is a being at once corporeal and spiritual.... Man, whole and entire, is therefore *willed* by God. (362)

> The human body shares in the dignity of "the image of God": it is a human body precisely because it is animated by a spiritual soul, and it is the whole human person that is intended to become, in the body of Christ, a temple of the Spirit. (364)

> The unity of soul and body is so profound that one has to consider the soul to be the "form" of the body: i.e., it is because of its spiritual soul that the body made of matter becomes a living, human body; spirit and matter, in man, are not two natures united, but rather their union forms a single nature. (365)

There are two temptations in our present age when

it comes to the body: to obsess over it or to ignore and neglect it. Neither is in line with the truth the Church teaches. We live in a world where the corporeal (a.k.a., flesh-and-bone, material) and the spiritual dimensions are inextricably linked, and God has called this good.

In fact, the Church goes so far as to tell us that we have to affirm the goodness of our bodies. In the Vatican II constitution *Gaudium et Spes*, we read:

> Man, though made of body and soul, is a unity. Through his very bodily condition he sums up in himself the elements of the material world. Through him they are thus brought to their highest perfection and can raise their voice in praise freely given to the Creator. For this reason man may not despise his bodily life. Rather he is obliged to regard his body as good and to hold it in honor since God has created it and will raise it up on the last day. (Quoted in CCC 364)

We cannot separate our body from our soul. The Church doesn't say anything about the size of the body or its physical health. The Church only tells us that the body is an integral part of who we are as human beings, created in God's image and likeness. Truly, I don't just *have* a body; in a very real sense I *am* my body.

Since the Scripture clearly tells us that God considers his creation good after he creates humans on the sixth day, who am I to say that my body is not good? Can I legitimately say that my body is excluded from the goodness of creation, even in its limitedness and weakness? Again, it comes back to the question of the purpose of my body, which is inextricably tied to the purpose of my soul. Therefore, when we consider

> Truly, I don't just *have* a body; in a very real sense I *am* my body.

the reasons God made humans, it must be an inquiry that considers the entire self of each human person, body and soul.

What is the purpose of the body?

Regarding the purpose and call of human beings, the *Catechism* says, "Of all visible creatures only man is 'able to know and love his creator.' He is 'the only creature on earth that God has willed for its own sake,' and he alone is called to share, by knowledge and love, in God's own life. It was for this end that he was created, and this is the fundamental reason for his dignity" (356).

The end, or purpose, of man is to have a relationship with God and to share in the life of God! This involves both soul and body. Not only must we make room for our relationship with God to involve body and soul, but we must also recognize that this is the key to the truth of the phrase "all bodies are good bodies."

> We were not created to be useful. We were not created merely to do things for God and for other people. We were created for a relationship with God, and any person — regardless of the state of their body — can have a relationship with God.

When we define the goodness of our body as its fitness, ability, size, strength, or absence of illness, we demonstrate that we don't understand the purpose for which God created each human being. We were not created to be useful. We were not created merely to do things for God and for other people. We were created for a relationship with God, and any person — regardless of the state of their body — can have a relationship with God. That is what makes a body good: the capacity for relationship with

God and with others. Therein lies its dignity. The *Catechism* continues:

> Being in the image of God the human individu-
> al possesses the dignity of a person, who is not
> just something, but someone. He is capable of
> self-knowledge, or self-possession and of freely giv-
> ing himself and entering into communion with
> other persons. And he is called by grace to a cov-
> enant with his Creator, to offer him a response of
> faith and love that no other creature can give in his
> stead. (357)

So what role does the body play in God's plan of sheer goodness? And what does this tell me about the goodness of my body? Our bodies are good because they enable us to have a relationship with the God who created us, and also with the precious people he has made and the beautiful world he has created. That means all bodies are good — sick or healthy, short or tall, abled or disabled or different-ly-abled, skinny or fat. Because no matter the state of my body, I can love God and receive his love for me. And so can you. We love the One who has let his own body be broken for us to have this relationship.

A special note

I need to address something important here: God has cre-ated us with a deep connection between our bodies and souls. It is impossible to sever this integration of body and soul completely, but because we are fallen and weak, the connection can be severely damaged. This connection was severely damaged in me, as a result of childhood abuse. My authority over my body was stolen by someone else's evil selfishness. The abuse I experienced has affected every part of who I am. My personal history led to an increased predilection for trying to live as though my body and my soul were completed disconnected. The sacraments of the Church have provided a refuge for me since my entrance into the Catholic Church several years ago. But the road to healing for me has also included hours of therapy. The life of God that flows through the Church and the power of the Holy Spirit to heal us are real, and God has given us wisdom to walk through healing from all sorts of pain. Sometimes that happens by simply continuing on in faith. But a lot of times, deep healing requires that we seek out the skills of a trained professional. If you have experienced trauma, please let yourself get help from a professional therapist who is trained in this area; it has been of immense help for me.

For reflection

Do I demand flawlessness of my body?

Do I believe that all bodies are good bodies? Why or why not?

In my life, how have I been tempted to separate my spiritual from my physical life? Do I see them as an integrated whole, or do I tend to focus on one, to the detriment of the other? What can I do to change that?

How is the truth that all bodies are good bodies a revelation of God's mercy?

Chapter 5

My Storied Body

"

*Every scar, every wound,
every ache inside of you
is a story. And stories are
the wildest, most powerful
things of all. Because stories
can build galaxies or make
entire universes break and
bleed and fall.*

"

NIKITA GILL, *YOU ARE MADE OF STORIES*

Saint John Paul II makes a pretty bold claim when he says, "The body reveals the person." It seems to contradict the story that I have been told my whole life as a fat girl — "It's what's on the inside that counts." But if John Paul II is right, what does my body reveal about my person? When I look in the mirror, I put the voice of criticism and self-loathing on mute, almost like I'm in a car turning the radio down so I can find the right house on the street. When the noise is gone, what can I see? This is my body. This is me.

There's the white mark on my right wrist from a surgery I had as a six-year-old. I tripped a lot as a kid and broke my fall with my wrists so many times that it required medical intervention. It makes me think of Saint Kateri Tekakwitha, whose first name is the French spelling of Catherine and whose second name in her indigenous language means "the one who bumps into things a lot." I definitely relate to her. Then there's the chicken pox scar in the middle of my forehead. It is a marker that I had the varicella virus instead of getting the vaccine as a kid in the '80s. (My children have all been vaccinated, so they won't get the joy of scratching themselves all over, unless it's from mosquitos.) I see my pale skin marked with freckles — proving my relation to my red-headed, freckled, Anglo mother, despite my Cuban heritage and surname — and my dark, curly hair from my father. I see my brown eyes, bright with joy and filled with a spark of mischief. And there are my arms that are quite muscular from holding my toddlers, and my legs that are even stronger from chasing after kids from morning to night. My belly hangs over the top of my legs and under the folds of skin, there is a long c-section scar where all four of my children made their debut into the light.

And then there are my feet. Hobbit feet — yes, with hair. Feet so flat that my footprint makes a triangle in-stead of that stereotypical curve where the arch is sup-posed to be. Feet so wide that I have to special-order

> If you turn down the volume on the voices of criticism and perfection and look in the mirror, your body is telling your story, too.

shoes to fit, and even then, it's iffy. Feet that took me through the joys and frustrations of gymnastics and cheerleading.

Every part of me. This is my body. This is me.

If you turn down the volume on the voices of criticism and perfection and look in the mirror, your body is telling your story, too. Take a look in the mirror (and if you have one, a full-length mirror). Notice what you see. Maybe you can write down snippets of the story your body tells. Your body is the keeper of your story, and it's a story worth telling.

Taken, blessed, broken, and given

Henri Nouwen, the late Dutch priest, professor, and theologian (1932–1996), lived a life of lonely brokenness. But he realized that his wounds could be a bridge between himself and the people around him, just as he met God through God's own wounds. Almost every book he wrote touched on this theme, that our wounds can bring healing to the world around us. In *Life of the Beloved*, Nouwen writes to a person who had asked him to explain more about life in the Spirit for those who did not have a background of faith.

Nouwen begins the book with the bold assertion that we, each and every person on earth, are beloved children of God, regardless of our personality, actions, or status. God loves us *simply because we exist*. (In fact, *we exist precisely because God loves us*.) Nouwen references the Scripture of Jesus' baptism, when heaven is opened and the Holy Spirit descends on him like a dove, and a voice from heaven declares, "You are my beloved Son; with you I am well pleased" (Lk 3:22). Nouwen asserts that we are as loved as Jesus is loved by the Father, with the ability to live as the Beloved of God. Each of us, Nouwen says, is taken, chosen uniquely and specifically to be loved. Each of us is *blessed* by God with unique talents and personalities and abilities. Each of us is *broken*, too, in a deeply personal way, whether by our circumstances, our own choices, or the violence and neglect of others in our lives.

But Nouwen doesn't simply end with a meditation on our brokenness, nor does he tell us to "count it all joy" and buck up in the midst of our sorrow. He goes on to show how each of us is uniquely given to the world — the people around us — through our chosenness, our blessedness, and our brokenness. I remember the moment that I realized that this Catholic professor-priest was laying out the pattern of my life: taken, blessed, broken, and given. He was describing me! And this is the pattern of the life of Jesus, too, which gives my joys and struggles a context of relationship and companionship. We are drawn into relationship with God, and this means we are also drawn into the story of the crucified God, who was taken, blessed, broken, and given for the salvation of the world.

The story that each of our bodies is telling has the same pattern. Can you see how your body has been chosen, blessed, broken, and given? To be honest, three of these descriptors are easy for me to identify in my life. I have nice Christian categories for God choosing my body, blessing my body, and giving my body for the sake of others. But that last one, being broken — how could that possibly be a good thing?

How can my brokenness be good? The answer to that question goes back to the concept of good that we discussed in the last chapter. A thing is good when it

fulfills its purpose. Nouwen's framework of being chosen, blessed, broken, and given enables us to ask the
question, "What am I being broken for? What is the
purpose of my brokenness?" Please hear me — I don't
mean that God wills for us to be broken; he doesn't. But
pain is an inevitable part of life as a human in this fallen
world, and we will inevitably possess brokenness within ourselves. The good news is God can use even our
brokenness for good. And we can see this brokenness
and know the story it tells. The very body of Jesus on
the cross tells us his story — nailed to a cross, crown of
thorns on his head, his side pierced by a spear.

Nouwen calls us to bring our brokenness under the
blessing of God, which is precisely what a crucifix does.
Instead of seeing a bloodied and pathetic man dying
a gruesome death (why would we want to see such a
crude image in every room of our homes and church-
es?) we see what love looks like: a holy man and a holy
God giving himself up to restore relationship with me,
his beloved. His body is broken for me. And this way
of seeing the crucifix brings the curse of the cross under the blessing. When brokenness is brought under the
blessing, it has meaning and purpose.

But our brokenness feels awkward and clunky, ugly
and painful. How can we bring all this pain and shame
and despair under the blessing? When we continue sitting in the shadows, afraid of the wounds we bear, hating ourselves for having them and rejecting ourselves,
we cannot live abundantly like Jesus promised. Only
when we invite the light to shine on us, to put our
wounds under the blessing, can we find peace and joy.

For reflection

Do I like the story my body tells? If yes, why? If no, why not?

Why is it important to lean into my body's role as the keeper of my story?

How can I place my brokenness under the blessing of God? How is this an act of mercy?

Chapter 6

My Weak Body

"To love at all is to be vulnerable. Love anything and your heart will certainly be wrung and possibly broken."

C. S. LEWIS

The dreaded pull-up bar. I hated seeing that thing, even when it was just in the corner being ignored during gym class. There were not many phrases I hated more in elementary school than "Presidential Physical Fitness Test." Thanks, LBJ, for making it harder to be a fat kid in public school. Someone thought, "This is a great way to promote health and fitness — a skills test (a competition, really) to show the physically superior students." Right. More like a literal test to separate the weak from the strong. How was this a good idea? Not only was I already subject to being called names because of my weight, I had to perform in front of the other kids in my class. I'm not super competitive, but I enjoy not sucking at physical activities. I mean, who likes being picked last for kickball? But there was something even more humiliating with the Presidential Physical Fitness Test. There were quotas. You were scored on how well you matched up to your peers, given a fail or a pass. I always failed. I felt humiliated.

And then there were cheerleading and gymnastics throughout elementary school and junior high. I wasn't particularly gifted, but both provided movement I enjoyed. I remember leaving cheerleading lessons as an eighth grader, and my feet were killing me. I had to limp very slowly and tenderly to the car. I was no stranger to foot pain; I can't remember a time in my life that my feet *haven't* hurt me. I should have questioned why this pain was so much worse than normal, but I thought it was just my body being weak. I was determined to power through it, because that is what I thought I needed to do. Foot pain was a weakness that I needed to conquer, and I had been told that the only way to defeat it was by losing weight. Cheerleading was a part of the strategy to lose weight, so I couldn't just quit. Turns out that I had stress fractures in two places in each of my feet. I thought my physical exertion and pain would diminish the weakness I saw in myself. Instead, it aggravated it. I wish I had listened to my body instead of the drive to eliminate my body's weakness.

Before becoming Catholic, my husband and I participated in the Rite of Christian Initiation of Adults (RCIA), a nine-month class to prepare us to be confirmed and to receive our first Holy Communion. Deacon Trevor and his wife Susan led our class through the teachings of the Catholic Church and answered questions that we had, but one lesson in particular stuck in my memory in a special way. Deacon Trevor shared the story of probably the most famous deacon in Church history, Saint Lawrence of Rome.

Lawrence was one of seven deacons in the Church at Rome in the second century, serving under Pope Sixtus II. Emperor Valerian was persecuting the Christians, and he had the pope and the other six deacons put to death, while Lawrence was told to go out and gather the treasures of the Church to hand over to the state. Lawrence was granted three days to do this, so he immediately began to distribute the gold and silver of the Church to the poor people in Rome. Then, he collected the sick, the disabled, and the wounded people of the Church and brought them with him back to the Roman authorities, saying, "These are the treasures of the Church!"

> What if my weakness is something to be treasured rather than despised?

The story of Saint Lawrence forced me to ask this question: What if my weakness is something to be treasured rather than despised?

Weak treasures

It's natural to see weakness in yourself and want to change it. But what happens when you try and try to change it, to prevent yourself from being weak and vulnerable, but you can't? How many diets have you started and stopped? How many exercise regimens have you sunk money into that didn't work for you? How much pain have you subjected yourself to in the pursuit of eliminating weakness from your body? It is so deeply ingrained in us that weakness is bad while strength is good. But we have to question that assumption, especially if weakness is something Jesus can use to draw us closer to him, even and especially weakness in our bodies.

Have you felt dragged down by a specific weakness in your body? Maybe you've prayed that God will take it away so that you can get on with your life. I know I have done that about the pain in my feet! What glorious things I might accomplish, I think, if I could move without pain! What is something you have asked the Lord to change about your body?

> The limitations of my body, whether they be my body's inability to perform or my horrible foot pain, tether me to Jesus.

Sometimes I wonder if the "thorn in the flesh" that Saint Paul speaks of in his second letter to the Corinthians is a physical ailment or weakness. I know for sure that I have pleaded more than three times for God to make me thin or to heal my feet. But listen to Jesus' response to Paul's pleas: "My grace is sufficient for you, for my power is made perfect in weakness" (2 Cor 12:8). Maybe you've heard this verse over and over again, but read it again slowly. Let it sink in. Jesus doesn't despise Paul's weakness. He knows it is a place where his power can be more fully revealed in his beloved. The limitations of my body, whether they be my body's inability to perform or my horrible foot pain, tether me to Jesus. His beautiful strength is made complete within me *through my weakness.* My weak body tethers me to Jesus. And if weakness ties me to Jesus, then maybe I don't have to despise it when I (inevitably) encounter it in myself.

A vulnerable God

Another word we use sometimes for weakness is "vulnerability." It comes from the Latin *vulnus*, meaning "wound." When something is vulnerable, it is able to be wounded. Human bodies are vulnerable. Yes, there are parts that are very strong — hands, arms, legs, shoulders, knees, elbows. These parts of our bodies are ready to make contact with something that might hurt us, like an elbow thrown up to protect our face from a bully's punch. (Or in my case, my hands thrown out in front of me to break my fall on the concrete when I trip.) But think about just how vulnerable certain parts of our bodies are — our stomachs, our throats, and even some that feel vulnerable just to mention, like breasts and testicles. Sometimes I wonder why God left us so vulnerable to physical harm. And then a question occurs to me: If we are created in the image of God, does our physical vulnerability indicate a vulnerability in God himself?

When I think about how Jesus made his entrance into the world in Judea, it baffles me. What kind of rescue operation depends on the survival of a helpless baby born to poor parents? But vulnerability is not an inconvenience for God; it's central to his *modus operandi*. In the story of the people of God, weakness and vulnerability are put on full display. A young virgin conceives out of wedlock? Super vulnerable. Forced to move during pregnancy? Giving birth far from home with your very recent husband? Fleeing a blood-thirsty ruler by taking refuge in a foreign country with a toddler? Just in the first two years of Jesus' life on earth, he encountered a ridiculously high volume of challenges to his vulnerability as a human child! When he began his ministry, he was as vulnerable as a homeless man, an itinerant preacher who depended on the generosity and hospitality of others. Even in his relationships, Jesus made himself vulnerable, letting Judas Iscariot into a place of deep friendship even though Jesus knew Judas would betray him. And then there's the vulnerability of dying on a cross. The vulnerability of a human being is on full display in the earthly life of Jesus of Nazareth. And if you think that Jesus' vulnerability ends after the Resurrection, think again.

The Wounded Lamb

The goal of a life with God is not the elimination of weakness or vulnerability. In his book *Strong and Weak*, Andy Crouch says that "when authority and vulnerability are combined, you find true flourishing." We don't have to despise our weak bodies, because Jesus shows us that authority and vulnerability can exist in holy tension. We can see that in the image of Jesus as the Wounded Lamb in Revelation 5. John sees some pretty powerful things, starting with God the Father seated on his throne, holding a seven-sealed scroll in his right hand. Everyone wants to know: What's in the scroll? Who is able to open it?

I imagine the scene: God the Father holds the mysterious scroll, surrounded by incredible creatures and twenty-four elders. A strong, shining angel, seeing the scroll in the Father's hands, asks loudly, "Who is worthy to open the scroll and to break its seals?" John falls to his knees with weeping because there is no one worthy of the task. One of the elders urges him, "Do not weep. The lion of the tribe of Judah, the root of David, has triumphed, enabling him to open the scroll with its seven seals."

I imagine John inhaling deeply, realizing that he *knows* this triumphant person, that he has leaned against the chest of the Lion of Judah, has been closer than a brother to the root of David. And then Jesus walks into view: *"And between the throne and the four living creatures and among the elders, I saw a Lamb standing, as though it had been slain."*

We know that Jesus is the Lamb of God — his own cousin proclaims this in John 1:29: "Behold, the Lamb of God who takes away the sin of the world!" And we hear this during every sacrifice of the Mass, right before the consecrated host, the body of the Lamb, is broken in two.

It is easy to think of Jesus as the slain lamb as he hangs on the cross at Passover. But in Revelation 5, it's not the crucifixion we behold — it's the wonderful aftermath: the crucified God-man, standing in glory. He bears the wounds of our salvation. They have not disappeared from his body, and in fact they mark his very identity: the slain-and-yet-standing Lamb. The wounded Lamb is the worthy one, the only one with the authority to open the scroll. And why does it matter that Jesus is the Wounded Lamb? I believe that the image of the Wounded Lamb is God showcasing two extremely important aspects of himself that exist simultaneously in tension: his vulnerability and his authority. With Jesus as our model, we don't have to avoid vulnerability or weakness at all costs. It's part of our destiny as the children of God to bear weakness and to let God's strength be made perfect in us.

> With Jesus as our model, we don't have to avoid vulnerability or weakness at all costs. It's part of our destiny as the children of God to bear weakness and to let God's strength be made perfect in us.

Adoration

The vulnerability of Jesus is why I love sitting before the Lord in the Blessed Sacrament in the adoration chapel. The broken body of Jesus made real in the Sacrament is Jesus at his most weak and vulnerable. His sacrifice is an eternal sacrifice, and when we participate in the Mass, we are actually participating in the crucifixion. Here is Jesus, in all his love and tenderness, offering himself up for us, inviting us to be close to him, inviting us to sit and wait with him. He is weak. And this is love.

The King of glory bears his wounds to his people —

authority and vulnerability in perfect balance. That is what is so beautiful about worshiping Jesus in the Blessed Sacrament. He doesn't expect us to come in strength and vigor. He receives us in all our weakness and woundedness. Our weakness is not a hindrance to communion with him; it is a tether that keeps us close to him. And all the places where we feel inadequate and unworthy, all the ways we fail to impress or succeed in this world, they are laid bare before him in love and vulnerability as we kneel before him. Like Jesus, we are taken, blessed, broken, and given. In our weakness, we abide with each other. And he fills us with joy and strength to walk in authority and vulnerability, sharing the good news of the Kingdom.

This passage comes to mind: "Since then we have a great high priest who has passed through the heavens, Jesus, the Son of God, let us hold fast our confession. For we have not a high priest who is unable to sympathize with our weaknesses, but one who in every respect has been tempted as we are, yet without sinning. Let us then with confidence draw near to the throne of grace, that we may receive mercy and find grace to help in time of need" (Heb 4:14–16).

As Christians, we recognize the authority of Jesus in conquering sin and death as he suffers and then rises on the third day. Can we recognize that when we join our sufferings to his, he gives us that same authority? It's not about lording over others; it's about fulfilling the mandate of creation to be fruitful and multiply and fill the face of the earth with humans who have a tender and strong relationship with their God. When we bear our vulnerability with authority, we minister to God and to his people.

The slain Lamb of God holds the fullness of the tension between authority and vulnerability in his very body, and this is cause for us to bow down and worship. But we don't bow down or cower in fear of an authoritarian God who demands perfection from us. No, we bow down to the tender, wounded God who has struggled in every way that we have and has shown us his powerful love by his death on the cross *and* his glorious resurrection.

The cross is the reality of God's love for us. It shows us that even in his weakness, God's love is stronger than death. And in the slain Lamb, we see that even in his victory, God does not despise the cross; he keeps his wounds visible for us.

We bear our wounds like he bears his, offering our love and bringing our weakness and woundedness under his beautiful blessing. We don't have to hide our scars. We can stand with authority and vulnerability contained in our bodies, confident that we participate in the beauty of God through our weak and frail bodies.

For reflection

Has my body disappointed me or let me down because of its weakness? Can I let Christ in to heal that memory?

Where can I exercise more authority over my physical life?

Have I allowed cultural perceptions or other people to convince me that I don't have such authority because of my size?

What does the reality of Jesus' weakness on the cross tell me about my own body in its perceived weaknesses?

How can I receive the mercy of God in my broken body?

Chapter 7

My Liturgical Body

"Man is a liturgical animal."

JAMES K. A. SMITH

Discovering that my body could be a weak body and still a good body was revolutionary for me. If this vulnerability that I carry in my body is a tether between me and Jesus, I can take a deep breath and rest in this body's goodness. Not only do I get to rest in my body's weakness and goodness, but I have a God-given authority over my body that I am learning to exercise. That's the other part of the tension — walking in the authority to which God has called us as his children. Based on the dignity we have in bearing the image of God, we do not have to submit our bodies to any authoritative influence that seeks to control us in our vulnerability, whether it be the cultural demands of perfection, the expectations of family members, or the voice in our head that tells us we're doing it all wrong.

I have found that I need to have a structure set up to help me in the day-to-day struggle of choices I'm presented with. There are lots of resources out there to develop your own rule of life, but what follows is how I have chosen to craft mine, exercising authority and maintaining vulnerability. I choose to call my rule of life a "personal liturgy." My friend Callie pointed out to me that the term "personal liturgy" seems like a contradiction, because the word "liturgy" derives from the Latin word that means "work of the people" — not just one person. She isn't wrong; a liturgy refers to a people, not merely a person. But the term "personal liturgy" is a reminder that how each of us lives our life in our body is meant for everyone. Absolutely, this personal liturgy is something I craft and control, but it is not strictly for myself. As followers of Jesus, we have the privilege of shaping our lives around the first two commandments:

> The term "personal liturgy" is a reminder that how each of us lives our life in our body is meant for everyone.

to love God with all we are and to love our neighbor as ourselves.

This work within each of us is a work *for the people — not just ourselves but our families, our friends, our neighbors, and our communities.*

Our culture's liturgy

In his 2009 book *Desiring the Kingdom: Worship, Worldview, and Cultural Formation,* Reformed Christian philosopher James K. A. Smith asserts that man is a liturgical animal. By that, he means that everything about human beings is influenced by the rhythms and rhymes we practice with our hearts, minds, souls, and bodies every day. He's on to something here, something the Church has known and practiced for millennia.

The word "liturgy" comes from the Greek λειτουργία (litourgia) and means "work of the people" or "public service." When we gather as a Church, we orient our lives a specific way to worship God. In Mass, we participate in the worship of the holy God in this work of the people that has been handed down to us through centuries of God-followers. While James K. A. Smith is not the first to think of man in terms of being a liturgical animal, his articulation can help us think about our daily lives as Catholic Christians. Every human, Smith claims, lives and breathes a liturgy. Each of us is shaped by the liturgy in which we live, for good or ill. Our assumptions, our predispositions, and our habits all reveal what we are oriented toward and reinforce our allegiance to that orientation.

So what is the prevailing liturgy of our culture? It is one of body control, perfection, flawlessness, where strength is celebrated and weakness brings shame. If we watch just a few ad cycles during our favorite show or see the sidebar ads on Facebook, what do we see? A new product for weight loss. A gym advertisement. An ad for plastic surgery. The latest healthy fad marketing. We are being bombarded with the rites and rituals of our culture's liturgy of health, fitness, and beauty. And we are unwittingly being formed by this messaging, which preaches discontentment with our appearance, skin, facial features, bodies, and dress size. We are so saturated with the propaganda that proclaims the superiority of thinness, health, and beauty that we don't even question it, not even as Christians who believe — supposedly — in the value of each individual no matter their ability, appearance, or attractiveness. Our culture has formed us in a liturgy of bodies that does not reflect the teachings of our faith, and it is our duty to question that liturgy. We have to let the teachings of Jesus and his Church confront the lies that thinness, health, and beauty are the markers of greatness or goodness.

When we are immersed in a liturgy of body hatred and condemnation of weakness, we — often unwittingly — begin to orient our lives around the perfect body, even though we are told to have no other gods before the Holy One of Israel. We settle for the status quo of our culture, hating our bodies if they reveal one ounce of weakness and beating them into submission, sometimes with literal violence. We obsess over how many grams of carbohydrates are dirtying our temples, or we make exercise a kind of god, placing our bodies on the scales of fitness and health. But this will never bring us peace.

Weight, size, and health

When people find out that I am a size-dignity activist, the question I get asked most often is some variation of this: "What about health?" The assumption is that since I claim that people should be treated with dignity no matter their size, I must be advocating for unhealthy lifestyles. But if it is true that our bodies were created for relationship with God and with the people around us, then we cannot ignore the full picture of health. Mentally and emotionally, we need serious help to maintain health. Diets and exercise regimens don't usually take this balance into account, and that can be dangerous for the people who practice them and prescribe them to their friends, family, and even patients.

Something that I have found helpful is Health At Every Size®, often referred to as HAES, an approach to health articulated by Dr. Linda Bacon (M.A. Exercise Science; Ph.D. Physiology). It is affirmed by the Association for Size Diversity and Health (ASDAH), which names the following HAES principles on its website (www.sizediversityandhealth.org):

- Weight inclusivity: size does not determine worth

- Health enhancement: all facets of health — physical, spiritual, emotional, mental — need attention

- Respectful care: addressing practices in ourselves and our culture that rob people of dignity regarding their bodies

- Eating for well-being (instead of for weight loss)

- Life-enhancing movement (rather than movement strictly for weight control)

In a nutshell, based on peer-reviewed studies, HAES rejects the assumption that weight or size are effective measurements of health. How much you weigh does not determine how healthy you are. So, if measures like the BMI, which is a ratio of height and weight, are not actually helpful in quantifying health, we look to measurements that are helpful, like blood pressure, blood sugar, and cholesterol levels.

As you think about and pursue health, remember that health includes more than just your physical health. Your spiritual, emotional, and mental health are also vital components of your health. Anyone who emphasizes one area to the detriment of the others is probably selling you something. For instance, it's interesting to note that in 2017, the weight loss industry was valued at over $60 billion.

I like to think of crafting my own liturgy as building a scaffolding around my habits, desires, fears, and dreams. There is a lot of vulnerability there, but this liturgy is an exercise in my God-given authority. A significant part of that scaffolding will be mapped out as you discern the vocation God has given you, whether it be as a person called to religious life, family life, or life lived in a community of friends. As you move to establish your own liturgy, consider framing it around these two questions:

> As you think about and pursue health, remember that health includes more than just your physical health.

- What practices will orient my heart toward a love of God and my neighbor as myself? (cf. Lk 10:27)

- How can I order my day so that I am seeking peace and pursuing it? (cf. Ps 34:14)

Going to the doctor

For a person who falls outside of the norms of culturally acceptable body size, going to the doctor can be an anxiety-producing event. As part of my personal liturgy, I have come up with ways to manage this anxiety so that I can have a peace-filled experience with my medical care rather than a panic attack in the waiting room (which has happened to me several times before). Here are the practices I have put into place to avoid that, and they might be helpful to you if you share these struggles.

Be prepared. Make a list of all your symptoms and any questions you have had about specific things, so you don't forget to ask or mention them due to nerves. I also bring a fully charged phone and a set of good earbuds with me for the lobby. There is usually a lot of information playing on loop that reinforces the cultural ideology of the body, so I avoid being inundated with messaging that tempts me to think poorly of my body.

> I urge you not to continue in anxiety and shame toward your body, fueled by a doctor's anti-fat bias.

Stand up for your body. If your health care provider suggests weight loss as a remedy to symptoms you describe, ask the following: "Do thin-to-average-size patients deal with these same symptoms?" If the answer is yes, then you can respond: "I'd like you to treat me as if I were one of them." Bias against fat people is clinically proven. Even doctors and nurses with kind hearts and good intentions can let their culturally formed intuition override what is the best care for their fat patients.

Standing up for my body looks like telling my doctor honestly that I am not focused on the number on the scale, and that I prefer to use the HAES approach — checking my blood pressure, my blood sugar, and my cholesterol levels instead of my weight. If they are not comfortable with approaching my medical care from this perspective, I know that I need to find another practitioner. Whatever you do, I urge you not to continue in anxiety and shame toward your body, fueled by a doctor's anti-fat bias. Your mental and emotional health are too valuable to be sacrificed on the altar of fat phobia. This is not being rude or naïve or dismissing reason; it is simply exercising authority over your body with kindness and firmness, in a way that brings you peace and health.

Bring an ally. When I find myself nervous about going

to an appointment by myself, I bring a friend. Usually my husband is able to come with me, which is what I prefer. Waiting for the doctor to come in is much easier when my husband is with me. For you, this person might be a sibling, a parent, or someone else who's close to you. Not only is it comforting, but having another person with you can be a buffer for potentially harmful situations.

Food is good

The words of Jesus in the Scriptures regarding food and peace puzzled me for a while. How could he be the bread of life *and* want to give me peace? Food and peace were at odds within me. In fact, if I had to name two entities in my childhood that I regarded equally with love and hate, they would be food and my appetite. I can't remember a time when my relationship to food was peaceful. I don't remember my life before dieting — I remember being urged to track my weight and to measure my portion sizes as early as age seven.

Being a people pleaser, it's no surprise that my desire to please others regarding my weight and food habits got all tangled up in the way I thought about my body, even in a religious context. Does this line of thinking sound familiar? "If my body is a temple of the Holy Spirit and it is too big to be a good or properly functioning body, maybe food is bad because it is making me fat." Our culture is really into the moralization of food, especially around the New Year when people are thinking about getting a fresh start on their body goals. In early December, our minds and hearts are flooded with advertisements and initiatives to be a "better you," which in common parlance means "a healthier (i.e., thinner) you." On social media, people I love can't stop talking about their diet regimens, full of "whole food" and "clean eating." This way of talking about food, though, is problematic.

In Acts 10, Peter is traveling to share the good news of

Jesus and performing miracles. He comes to Joppa and rais-
es a righteous woman, Tabitha, back to life. He decides to
stay in Joppa a little while in the home of Simon the tanner,
presumably to continue to share the Gospel and to spend
time with the new Christians there. While he is staying at
Simon's home, he escapes to the roof to have some time
alone to pray, and there God gives him a vision.

> Peter went up on the housetop to pray, about the
> sixth hour. And he became hungry and desired
> something to eat; but while they were preparing
> it, he fell into a trance and saw the heaven opened,
> and something descending, like a great sheet, let
> down by four corners upon the earth. In it were
> all kinds of animals and reptiles and birds of the
> air. And there came a voice to him, "Rise, Peter;
> kill and eat." But Peter said, "No, Lord; for I have
> never eaten anything that is common or unclean."
> And the voice came to him again a second time,
> "What God has cleansed, you must not call com-
> mon." This happened three times, and the thing
> was taken up at once to heaven. (Acts 10:9b–16)

God is redirecting the words that Peter uses to refer to
his food. The Jews had a very strict way of eating according
to Levitical law. See for instance Leviticus 11:47, which en-
capsulates the rules surrounding food: *"to make a distinction
between the unclean and the clean and between the living creature
that may be eaten and the living creature that may not be eaten."*

Peter had always been a faithful Jew, so he naturally put
a lot of stock into eating cleanly. For Peter and his fellow
Jews, eating practices were a large part of what defined a
person. The Jews ate one way — a very specific way, given
to them by God. In this scene, when Peter protests against
eating these unclean animals, he uses the words he learned
from the Scripture and his culture: *"I have never eaten anything common or unclean"* (Acts 10:14).

Yet God responds with a strong counterstatement: "Rise, Peter; kill and eat. ... What God has cleansed you must not call common."

Peter's encounter with the sheet full of animals is framed by another story. Acts 10 opens with the story of Cornelius, "a centurion of what was known as the Italian Cohort, a devout man who feared God with all his household, gave alms liberally to the people, and prayed constantly to God" (10:1–2). Right before Peter has his vision, Cornelius has one of his own, in which God tells him to go find Peter. He obeys and sends his men to bring Peter to him.

> The way we talk about food is without a doubt connected to the way we view the people who eat certain foods.

There's just a slight problem — Cornelius is a Gentile, and Peter is a Jew. At this point in history, in this part of the world, these two groups don't really mix. But Peter has just had a curious encounter with God, and he listens to the voice of the Holy Spirit that tells him, "Behold, three men are looking for you. Rise and go down, and accompany them without hesitation; for I have sent them" (10:19–20).

Peter welcomes them in and the next day they journey back to Cornelius. When Peter meets Cornelius, he says something really important: "You yourselves know how unlawful it is for a Jew to associate with or to visit any one of another nation; but God has shown me that I should not call any man common or unclean" (10:28).

Why is this important? Because Peter recognizes that the vision he received about food goes much deeper than mere dietary restrictions. By redefining how his people are to eat, God is saying something really important about humans and the way we are to relate to one another. And isn't it true? *For whatever reason, the way we talk about food is without a doubt connected to the way we view the people who eat certain foods.*

Therefore, we can see that it is no small thing to make the jump from "clean eating and unclean eating" to "clean people and unclean people." This was a defining mark in the Jewish tradition — how you ate determined your inclusion or exclusion.

We see this dynamic at play in American culture, for sure. The phrase "eating clean" is currently popular, but the same idea is expressed in many ways: eating healthy, eating right, eating whole. It's not that these terms are bad in themselves, and I readily admit that it's hard to think of talking about health and food in other terms.

Yet because we are called to love our neighbors, we must be careful of the implications of the way we talk about food and self-care. Here's just one example: What if you're not eating "clean"? Then you must be eating dirty. And because our culture defines us by how we eat (and this is also reflected in Peter's experience in Jewish culture), people who don't eat clean aren't clean. They are dirty. They are unhealthy. They are not whole. In a culture that clings tightly to the idea that you are what you eat, there is a social disgust for certain foods and the people who partake of them. Just think about the images of fat people you see on news reports, maybe buying pizza or burgers, their headless bodies waddling around a mall food court. That is not dignity. That is dehumanizing. For our own sake and for the sake of our neighbors created in God's image, we cannot let how someone eats define their personhood. What God has called clean — in food and in people — we cannot call unclean.*

Equipped for eating

What should we do, then, in a culture that makes eating so complicated? Eating is such a vulnerable activity. How

---

* This section was modified from a post that originally appeared at amandamartinezbeck.com.

can we exercise authority over the food we eat in a way that brings us peace? Intuitive eating is a concept I have found helpful on the journey of making peace with food. One of the foundations of intuitive eating is that when we are born, our bodies know what we need when it comes to nutrition, including when to eat, how much to eat, and what to eat. As we grow, the people and the culture around us can cause us to mistrust our bodies' signals, and we lose that God-given intuition. Intuitive eating is a process that encourages you to be mindful of what your body is communicating to you about your nutritional needs rather than following the manmade rules of diet culture. I suggest starting with the book *Intuitive Eating* (2012) by registered dietitians Evelyn Tribole and Elyse Resch.

Joyful movement

I remember hearing my pastor in college refer to his body as a "flesh-can."

The disgust and frustration evident in his voice as he spoke of his body was not new to me; in fact, it was the way I'd heard bodies spoken of within Christian contexts for my whole life. The pastor went on to discuss his running regimen and how, to quote Saint Paul, he "beat his body into submission" for the sake of the Gospel. I looked down at my body and knew that it was clear that I had done no such thing. If I had, I wouldn't be wearing plus sizes. The way he talked about his body being a trash can of flesh confirmed what I felt about my body, and I wondered how God could use me to bring his kingdom to earth if I couldn't even take care of this sorry body of mine.

While I think the goal of my college pastor was to encourage self-discipline in relation to exercise and spirituality, the message I heard was that until I'm exercising and beating my body into submission, I'm going to lose the race toward spiritual maturity. What good does it do me to think about moving my body in this way? The fruit of this way of thinking is rotten. In my life, it has produced nothing but a sense of failure and shame because I feel like I have let God down with my lack of exercising. I've found much more peace and freedom when I approach movement as a joy rather than an obligation.

When thinking about your body and how it moves, consider two things. First, movement can be joyful! It does not have to be a task where calories, or even distance, is measured. You can move for the sake of the joy that it brings you. For me, I love to dance. Maybe you like the treadmill or swimming. Here's a challenge: find a movement that brings you joy and don't look at its "benefits" related to calories burned or some distance goal.

> **Movement can be joyful!**

Second, movement can build and strengthen community. You can get your body moving in certain ways that knit you together in relationship with others. Maybe that means joining a neighborhood walking group or a class at the gym. Maybe that means volunteering to chase after kids at Vacation Bible School or to coach a little league team. To enjoy movement, I get the focus off myself and the "results" of exercising, and I do something that builds relationships with the people around me. I love to throw on some music with a beat and have a dance party with my kids!

Think about the movement that brings you joy and practice it just for fun. How can you use joyful movement to build relationships with the people around you?

Clothing

For many people — my oldest daughter included — getting dressed is an artistic activity. During the school day, my daughter is required to wear her school uniform. When she is home from school, though, it is important to me that she has creative authority over her wardrobe. That often means that she chooses something to wear that I would not have thought of. But this exercise in her authority is much more valuable and important for her than my expectations of what a well-dressed kindergartner is. (And watching her style develop is truly a delight!) Even when she wears her uniform, I try to let her exercise as much authority as possible — her headbands, hairstyles, and choice of shoes are up to her, and that's a good thing. Yes, my five-year-old picked out five headbands to wear at once. And I love it.

As my daughter and I delight in the process of clothing ourselves, our understanding of clothing adapts, changes, deepens. Clothing is for so much more than strategically hiding parts of our bodies. In our society, we are given so many rules about what we can wear. In the fashion world, horizontal stripes are a no-no for big girls, and tight-fitting clothes are culturally reserved for thin, toned bodies with no rolls or dimples. In many Christian circles, Catholic and Protestant alike, modesty is the rule for women and girls. But modesty is such a subjective concept, and the battle over clothing, more often than not, shows itself to be a battle for control that usurps the God-given authority of a person to dress themselves in a way that reveals their personality and cultivates joy.

> Clothing is for so much more than strategically hiding parts of our bodies.

In my journey to embrace the body God gave me, claiming authority over my wardrobe has been vital to the process. For far too long, advice like "Black is slimming" and "Hide your belly pooch" kept me concealing the big parts of myself. Now, instead of using clothing to hide perceived flaws in my body, I dress to reveal — not my skin or sex appeal, but my personality. Pretty dresses, form-fitting or flowing. Skin-tight leggings and my favorite t-shirt. And colors! Prints! Patterns! I'm not hiding anymore.

J. Nicole Morgan, my friend and the author of *Fat and Faithful* (Fortress Press, 2018) encouraged me to wear my personality in a bold way through makeup, too. She chooses beautiful shades of lipstick, depending on the outfit she's sporting. Her Instagram — filled with lipstick selfies and fat hiking photos — is an inspiration to me. "I like that when I wear lipstick, it stays behind. It leaves a mark," Nicole explained on the podcast we co-host, *Fat & Faithful.* Like Nicole with her lipstick, I choose to reject the cultural pressure to be a quiet fat girl who fades into the background to avoid commentary on my body. My fashion choices, from fun dresses to strappy Chacos to dazzling lip color, are an exercise of my authority over myself, and I love it!

If you feel yourself getting nervous about clothes shopping, take a deep breath. Follow some fashionistas on Instagram who have a similar body type to yours. See your body as something to be clothed with intention and delight, not something to be hidden out of shame. Order that top you've been eyeing online. You can return it if it doesn't fit the way you want. If you go to a brick-and-mortar store, take a trusted friend. Let the creativity you were born with flow through to your clothing choices.

Following God in truth

As you craft your personal liturgy, remember — you have authority here. Know what you as a whole person need. If you think it would be beneficial, find a therapist to help get you on the path to mental health. Find a dietician who teaches intuitive eating rather than dieting. Find a doctor who practices HAES. Eat in a way that brings you peace. For every component of your health, do what brings you peace, mentally and emotionally *and* physically and spiritually. It's not predictable and it's not scientific, but it is about relationship (with ourselves, with others, and with God), not a performance or metric.

However you choose to craft yours, each of us should

see our personal liturgy as beginning with orienting our life toward the greatest two commandments: to love God and to love our neighbor as ourselves. The first part of that — loving God — comes first of all through a vibrant relationship with him and his Church through a sacramental life. So much of the liturgy of today's culture is oriented toward personal success and a misguided idea of perfection, while leaving the weak, underperforming, and marginalized behind. The waters here are murky, full of messaging that runs counter to the message of love that we hear from God, read in the Scriptures, and see through the testimony of the Church. God has created our bodies for a relationship with him, not for rules that will lead us to a smaller number on the scale or a tummy that doesn't bulge.

Ultimately, the Liturgy of the Church is a bulwark for us. The smells and bells, as some call them, tether us to the reality of God's kingdom. I can't retreat and "do church" on my own, because my body and my soul need what the physical Church gives to me: the forgiveness of sins, the hope of heaven, and the true food and true drink of the Bread of Life.

We must let our intuition about bodies be shaped by the Holy Spirit rather than by the cultural liturgy. This is an intentional endeavor, one that demands joy and peace, not fear. If we can change our mind-set toward the body from one of whipping it into submission to one of rejoicing in its eternal goal of relationship with God, we can find joy and peace as we figure out what works and what doesn't in our personal liturgy. As

> I can't retreat and "do church" on my own, because my body and my soul need what the physical Church gives to me: the forgiveness of sins, the hope of heaven, and the true food and true drink of the Bread of Life.

long as our hearts are set toward a loving relationship with God and a passion to love and serve our neighbor, we can pursue peace for our bodies without fear.

For reflection

What key elements will my personal liturgy include? How can I incorporate mercy into it?

How can I push back against the cultural liturgy, with its focus on the "perfect" body? How can I do this without anger or defensiveness, but in Christian charity?

Chapter 8

My Sacramental Body

"Man is a hungry being. But he is hungry for God."

ALEXANDER SCHMEMANN

When I was very young, my parents and I attended Odessa Bible Church in west Texas. Every week, the pastor would lead the congregation in communion, passing out little pieces of cracker and little cups of grape juice as he told us to remember Jesus' sacrifice for us through these symbols. I was three years old, and as my parents tell it, I was very eager to take part in communion.

I tried to help myself to the trayful of crackers as it was passed in front of me, but my parents stopped me. On the way home from church, they explained that communion was for those people who had received Jesus into their hearts. They told me about the problem of sin and the need for a savior. That afternoon, I prayed a three-year-old's prayer to invite Jesus into my life.

When we went to church the next Sunday, I was ready to eat my cracker and drink my juice! As the elements were passed around, my parents almost didn't let me participate. They weren't sure that I had really known what I had prayed the week before, because I was so young. In no uncertain terms, I let them know that I hadn't missed the point. When they kept the crackers from me, I exclaimed, very loudly so everyone in the church could hear, "I believe that Jesus died on the cross for my sins, and I want to take communion!"

This story of my decision to trust Jesus should be filled with nothing but joy. But for a long time, I was ashamed of it. I saw my big appetite as a negative thing that had ruined a part of my life. Later, as I began my journey into the Catholic Church, I realized that from my early childhood, God had been using my appetite to draw me to himself. My appetite — along with the other needs and desires of my body — is not my enemy. No, my needs and desires tether me to God and draw me into life with him.

The sacraments and you

I had never really considered the sacramental nature of our

world until a professor invited me to. He encouraged me to think about the beauty, danger, and significance of a world that points me to God. Suddenly, every flower spoke to me and every tree told a story. Has this happened to you? Maybe you've had an encounter with God in nature. Perhaps it hasn't occurred to you until now that the peace and satisfaction you were feeling then was God connecting with you. These experiences can be salve to a weary soul. When one happens to me, I savor it. I've come to learn that encounters like these come and go. And I've found that as much as I value them, I value even more that the sacraments are always available for us to connect with God through our body and soul — even if we don't necessarily feel it. What an amazing existence we enjoy — to have the sacraments as an outward and visible sign of an inward and spiritual grace given to us by God!

> The sacraments are always available for us to connect with God through our body and soul — even if we don't necessarily feel it.

Consider the role of water in our life, both physically and spiritually. It covers most of the earth, it makes up most of our cells, and it is vital to our survival. We are baptized into the Faith with water, we mark ourselves with it when we enter the Church, and we watch the priest wash his hands before the consecration of the Eucharist. In the Old Testament, the prophet Ezekiel hears the voice of God and it sounds like "the sound of mighty waters" (Ez 43:2). In Revelation, Saint John describes Jesus' voice as "the sound of many waters" (Rev 1:15). I can't help but connect these descriptions of the voice of God to the waters of baptism. The sacramental nature of water is hauntingly beautiful. Even when I stand in the shower and let the water flow down over my head, I sometimes sense the voice of God proclaiming his delight over me, like he did over Jesus at his baptism, saying, "You are my Son, the Beloved; with you I am well pleased" (Lk 3:22).

Our faith shows us how intimately connected our bodies are to our relationship with God. Each of the sacraments knits us into the Body of Christ through our physical participation. In baptism, the water of life washes us of original sin. In the Eucharist, we consume the Body and Blood of Jesus. In confession, we use our voices to confess our sins and our ears to hear the comforting words of forgiveness. Reconciliation requires us to be fully present, body and soul. Physically getting to a confessional is an act that requires our body, and confessing our sins, receiving forgiveness, and even performing our penance affects us body and soul. In confirmation, the chrism oil marks us as those who have been sealed by the Holy Spirit. The anointing of the sick involves the laying on of hands for our healing. And holy orders and matrimony involve dedicating our entire selves, body and soul, to a very specific calling.

To put it in a humorous way — if you want to be Catholic, you have to have a body! How has your body been a part of your relationship with Jesus and his Church?

Total physical response

When I was teaching Spanish in the classroom, I employed a strategy called "total physical response," or TPR for short. The premise of TPR is that if we put our language learning into practice through our bodies, we remember it better and internalize the language lesson. Kids do it all the time as they learn their own native language — think about how many raucous renditions of "Head, Shoulders, Knees, and Toes" your preschool teacher led you through! I've found that the same is true in the life of a Christian: we need a total physical response if we are to learn the life-giving truth of the Church. If we can't practice with our bodies as we learn new things (whether it be language with our lips or philosophy with our day planners), odds are that we won't learn it deep down in our hearts. And in fact, a life with God *must* be about heart, mind, soul, and body — not simply about head knowledge. The sacraments of the Church reveal how knit together our bodies and souls are, and they help us live out that integration with grace.

Think of how *physical* the sacraments are! The union of matrimony has the power to bring forth new human life, filling the air with the cries of a newborn. The waters of baptism get us good and wet, washing our skin and setting our hearts toward God. The bread and wine of the Eucharist literally feed us. The chrism oil marks us with its holy scent for the sacraments of confirmation, holy orders, and the viaticum (last rites). Our knees feel the weight of our whole bodies as we kneel in the confessional. The sacraments connect us body and soul to God, and I am sure that God didn't do that by accident. If you've ever seen the joy of a child getting sprinkled with holy water during a blessing, you can see a glimpse of the joy of this sacramental life we were made for.

> The sacraments connect us body and soul to God, and I am sure that God didn't do that by accident.

The *Catechism* says that "the seven sacraments are the signs and instruments by which the Holy Spirit spreads the grace of Christ the head throughout the Church which is his Body" (774). It continues: "The sacraments are perceptible signs (words and actions) accessible to our human nature. By the action of Christ and the power of the Holy Spirit they make present efficaciously the grace that they signify" (1084). Furthermore,

> the Church's mission is not an addition to that of Christ and the Holy Spirit, but is its sacrament: in her whole being and in all her members, the Church is sent to announce, bear witness, make present, and spread the mystery of the communion of the Holy

Trinity. ... Because the Holy Spirit is the anointing of Christ, it is Christ who, as the head of the Body, pours out the Spirit among his members to nourish, heal, and organize them in their mutual functions, to give them life, send them to bear witness, and associate them to his self-offering to the Father and to his intercession for the whole world. Through the Church's sacraments, Christ communicates his Holy and sanctifying Spirit to the members of his Body. (738–39)

Have you read in 1 Samuel, when Samuel the prophet anoints David as king over Israel? Can you imagine the scene? An old man with a horn of oil pours it over the young shepherd's head. It is messy. The fragrance is thick, and it runs through his ruddy hair down his cheeks and through his beard and onto his chest. I wonder what David's face looked like when this occurred; I can only imagine his simultaneous confusion, delight, and surprise. This wasn't just a word of prophecy spoken; it was a physical act, the memory of which I'm sure David kept in his heart forever. I imagine the sacraments in a similar way, except that Jesus is the one anointing his Bride the Church with the oil that is the Holy Spirit. It is fragrant; it is wet; it is messy. And week after week, we participate in the life of God through the sacraments as they make his life available to us.

In proclaiming the efficacy and necessity of the sacraments for the life of faith, the Catholic Church stands against the temptation toward dualism that each human faces. Our faith leads us to recognize the inseparability of our body and soul, because the sacraments are not merely symbols. Something powerful is happening, showing clearly that what we do in the flesh matters for our souls. It cannot be understated how important the sacraments are to living life with God and his people. They have been a part of the life of the Church since Jesus Christ instituted them himself, and we need them in order to be knit in.

Sacramental living

As Catholics, we have no lack of practices that help us live out the sacraments. The Eucharist is available on a daily basis for most of us! Regular confession and daily examination of conscience are vital and very practical. And even the simple act of blessing ourselves with holy water allows us to lean into the graces of our baptism. Take the opportunity to remind yourself, body and soul, that you have been buried with Jesus in baptism and raised to walk in newness of life, sealed by the Holy Spirit through confirmation!

The Incarnation and our bodies

The doctrine of the Incarnation is utterly marvelous, but how many of us take the time to stop and ponder it? God took on flesh to be our brother and to save us. God didn't leave fallen humans in their sin to die without him. Instead, the Second Person of the Trinity became a man, taking on body and soul, to save us, body and soul. The Incarnation is the ultimate affirmation of the goodness of every human body!

If Jesus is perfect God *and* perfect man, then each of us must examine the implications for our flesh. Just consider the body of Jesus as he lived on earth. Think about Jesus as a baby and the sweet little fingers and toes he must have had. Think about Jesus as a young boy testing the power of his arms and legs as he ran through the Judean countryside. Think about Jesus as a man in the home of the scribe as Mary Magdalene washed his feet with her tears and dried them with her hair. Jesus was a man who lived with a body, healed people with his touch, who got dirty and took baths and went to the bathroom daily and blew his nose! And there is no way we can see his body as anything but good. If the physical body of Jesus is good, what does this mean for our physical bodies? In the Incarnation, God affirmed the goodness of creation. Our bodies are a part of that created goodness.

Recently, after receiving the Eucharist at Mass, as I made my way back to my seat, I passed a woman sitting at the edge of her pew, hands extended in expectation. I glanced behind me and saw the green robes of the deacon flowing toward her. I noticed a cane next to the woman and her hands held in position to receive the body of our Lord. She couldn't make it to the front of the church to take the Eucharist, and that was okay. Jesus met her where she was, her aging body still good despite her physical limitations. She received Jesus into her mouth and her heart, knit together with the Body of Christ through the sacrament of the Eucharist. If, as we discussed in chapter 4, the purpose of a body is to have a relationship with God and with our neighbor, then the sacraments highlight this: no matter the condition of our body — frail, wounded, chronically ill, skinny, or fat — we can have a dynamic relationship with God, through the sacraments that he has given his Church, alongside our neighbors.

For reflection

Do I see my life as a sacramental life?

What does participation in the sacraments of the Church mean to me? How has it changed me?

How can I be more aware of my body's role in my relationship with God?

How do the sacraments reveal the mercy of God to my body?

Chapter 9

My Neighbor's Body

"Love of Christ does not distract us from interest in others, but rather invites us to responsibility for them, to the exclusion of no one and indeed, if anything, with a special concern for the weakest and the suffering."

POPE SAINT JOHN PAUL THE GREAT

One day I was carrying my daughter Lucy into the house from the car. She leaned her head against my shoulder and began to pat my back with her little hand. The experience brought tears to my eyes because I never taught her that — she was just giving me comfort in the way she had received it. How many times had I picked up her and wiped her tears, then walked her around the living room, patting her back and telling her that she was going to be okay?

Lucy was giving me affection and comfort in the way I had modeled it to her. It's how we're wired to learn, by observing those we spend time with and imitating them. Our words and actions toward our bodies are part of this wiring, too. It follows that the attitude with which I approach my own body will teach my daughters and son how to approach their own. And I know I'm not the first one to say it, but the truth is unavoidable: we can't give mercy unless we have received it for ourselves. If I want to teach my children to extend mercy to their bodies, I must receive mercy for my body first. This lesson is so important in the journey to embracing all bodies as good, because if I haven't given my own body the mercy and kindness it deserves, I will not be able to give these things consistently to others. How I live in my body — how hospitable I am to my own person — is reflected to the people around me. In my life, it's what I like to call "fat hospitality." It's the principle that when I make a welcoming place within myself and in my home for me to take up as much space as my body needs, I am ready to receive others with the same love and mercy.

> If I haven't given my own body the mercy and kindness it deserves, I will not be able to give these things consistently to others.

Countering hostility with hospitality

More often than not, this world does not offer hospitality to people who don't conform to our culture's expectations of bodies. Those of us who defy these expectations walk around in a world that is hostile to us, unsafe, unwelcoming, and exhausting. Each of us needs a safe space to just *be ourselves.* But if I don't cultivate this space for my own body, I am unable to offer it to others — because we can only offer comfort to others that we have truly received for ourselves.

> Failure to learn the lesson that all bodies are good bodies affects our neighbors — even when the body that we refuse to accept is our own.

When it comes to our bodies, we have to come near the throne of grace so that we can receive mercy when we need it. Then we are called to turn our focus outward, to put Romans 15:7 into practice in our lives: "Welcome one another, then, as Christ has welcomed you, for the glory of God." This is Christian hospitality: pouring out the mercy we have received from God to those around us. When it comes to bodies, it means saying "no" to cultural standards that promote violence, abuse, and neglect of bodies that don't fit the accepted norm. It means rejecting words, attitudes, and practices that dehumanize our neighbors and assign morality to food choices, exercise habits, or physical health. It means being deeply pro-life and knowing that when we celebrate our body as good in its weakness, we create a space of refuge for the weakness of others — the elderly, the sick, the unborn, and the poor.

Failure to learn the lesson that all bodies are good bodies affects our neighbors — even when the body that we refuse to accept is our own. Our critical words and self-hatred can cause others to wonder if we see their broken and weak bodies in the same way. They may conclude that we consider them worthy of hatred and condemnation for the imperfections in their bodies, whatever those imperfections might be. (I know how I have felt when an average-sized friend complains about how fat she is, when I'm obviously much bigger than she is.) The journey to embracing this body God has given me is about so much more than just me; it's about being able to love my neighbor well. And if I hate myself, loving my neighbor as much as I love myself will not leave them with much.

Losing perspective

I will say it again: recognizing that my body is good isn't just about me. It turns me outward, toward the precious people around me. Every person I encounter is deeply loved, deserving of dignity and welcome. But when I make assumptions about a person based on their size — whether they be bigger or smaller than I am — I easily lose perspective.

Recently, I was at a conference when I had one of those days where the feeling of my own insignificance pressed down and was crushing me. I struggled to see my worth and value in just about every area of my life: as a wife and mother, as a friend, as a professional. Self-doubt and insecurity stuck with me for days, and the thoughts of my own inferiority flooded my brain.

Why would anyone want to hear what I have to say? What if I fail? What if all this time and effort have been for nothing? What if I am wasting my life?

I tried to practice mindfulness. I tried to quiet my soul and hear the still, soft voice of our loving God speak peace to me. But the static of doubt and insecurity was too distracting. I tearfully tried to explain what was wrong to a friend. I tried to explain how my size was a hindrance to helping people. I shared how I was exhausted from fighting the stereotypes against fat people and that I didn't know if I was up to the task. As we talked through my pain, I came to realize that I had been comparing my body to the others around me, and this comparison had stolen my perspective. I knew that the purpose of my body was to have a relationship with God and with my neighbors, but I had drifted from the truth. Seeing bodies that the world perceives as "better" than mine, I became jealous of the ease with which those people seemed to move through life. I coveted their bodies. But the reality is that having a different body would not change my capacity for relationship or my ability to love or serve others. It wasn't my body that was limiting my ability to love and serve for others; it was my wishing to have a different body that distracted me from it.

> Accepting that my body is lovely and good is a fight that requires perseverance. It is not done in a day, a month, or even a year.

Accepting that my body is lovely and good is a fight that requires perseverance. It is not done in a day, a month, or even a year. It's a pilgrimage to get to the place where my perception of my body equals God's perception of my body. There have been so many times when I've wanted to quit this pilgrimage, to go back to hating my body and to let our culture define my worth based on my size. It may be a rotten existence dwelling in self-loathing, but at least it's familiar. But every time I'm tempted to go back down that path, I remember: my body is good and tells a story of the faithfulness of God. As I travel toward loving my body like God does, others see the changes and the hope that he is putting in me. They see the truth that is setting me free from a life of slavery to expectations of body perfection. In all these places, I can see that recognizing that my body is good isn't just about me.

That day at the conference, when believing that my body

was good seemed too hard and I contemplated giving up, my friend looked me in the eye and said, "Amanda, will you keep going for the people who are like you, the ones who don't think there is a place for them? Will you push through the hard parts and the pain and the rejection so that you can stand in front of them and tell them it is possible?"

I had to choke back the tears as I realized this truth: showing up with love and joy for the people around you — doing little things with great love — that is what changes the world. And I can do that whether I'm skinny or fat or average, whether my body works like it's "supposed" to or not. I am not insignificant. I matter. I have something to say. And so do you. As we come to the end of this journey, I hope you can hear this: you have something to say, and if you don't say it, no one ever will. And the world will be the lesser for it.

For reflection

How does receiving the mercy of God for my body affect the mercy I can offer to others?

Have I judged people based on their bodies, whether they are the same or different from me?

Do I recognize that all bodies are good bodies, not just mine, but the bodies of those around me? Do I live as though I recognize this?

How can I practice real hospitality to everyone I encounter? What might need to change in me to make this encounter possible?

Conclusion

While I was at that conference, the siren song of our culture's body expectations filled my head and made me lose perspective. Something happened, though, that changed the song my heart was singing. It was late, and my friends and I were driving to a party after the last conference session of the evening. Ever the mom, I pestered the driver to buckle up for the short commute. Two minutes later, we were hit from behind. We were shaken, but physically we were okay. The woman who had rear-ended us, however, was injured. She was pregnant and had a five-year-old child in the backseat. As the paramedics wheeled the mother into the ambulance, the little girl sat in shock. The police asked us questions, and I held the little girl. In my large body with soft curves and messed up feet, I sat on the curb and rocked her. I sang her Cuban lullabies when I learned that her dad was Cuban, like mine. She let me hold her for a long time, and as I rocked and sang, I thought of my four babies at home. On a Friday night under bright street lights, this little one rested in my arms. I thought of how privileged I was to be there at that moment, fully present for this child, in my good body.

This is what changes the world. Each of us being fully present in our imperfect and yet good bodies.

In my life, what does that look like? It's me, singing Cuban lullabies to a little girl I've never met before and will likely never meet again. Me, loving my children with this large body, kissing booboos and letting them bury their heads into my soft curves. Me, being fully present to my husband when I am tempted to hide myself because of my size. It means learning to sing my song, the one of love for God and this good body he has given me. The verses are filled with memories I've let myself remember, and the chorus is about my good body that has the capacity for love in this hurting world. It is a song of loving and of being loved. It is a song of this good body and the story that it is telling. It is a song of freedom. It is a song of joy.

You also have a song, but maybe you have never been

able to hear it above the sirens of our culture. Listen for it now. Its rhythm is beating within you, too. When you join in the singing, the song of freedom gets louder. I see us, you and me, walking together, holding Mary's hand as she follows Jesus. We sing the song of the mercy of God, and all who hear our voices are invited in to a place where they are free to be themselves, right now, in the body God has given them. As we go into the world, we remember the stories that our bodies are telling. We sing of our wounds. We sing of our victories. We sing of the sacraments that knit us into the Body of Jesus, his Church. It is a song of mercy, and its refrain is sweet and brings us peace.

Your voice is needed in this song, because you are created in the image of the Creator. The works of art we create when we orient our lives toward God and our neighbor will change the world. When we can say with honesty that all bodies are good bodies, when we can start to love the body that God gave us and know that this love is a radical declaration of God's kingdom, things really get exciting. We bring our creative energy to bear on the redemption of the world. We can say "no" to the lies that hold us back and keep us down. We can walk in freedom and truth. We can sing with confidence to our spouses, our friends, our children, our neighbors, and even our enemies, the refrain that draws us into fellowship with each other, all of us full of vulnerability and authority: *Your body is good, and I love the story that it's telling.*

About the Author

AMANDA MARTINEZ BECK is an author and story consultant who lives with her husband, Zachary, and their four young children in the Piney Woods of East Texas. An adult convert to the Catholic Faith, she is fluent in both Evangelical Protestant and Catholic vernacular, doing translating work where it is needed. Amanda is a size-dignity activist and writes to help people see the truth that all bodies are good bodies, no exceptions. She is the Catholic half of the size-acceptance duo that hosts the podcast *Fat & Faithful*, and her goal is to help others accept their bodies as good so that they can love their neighbors as themselves and change the world. She is on Instagram (@your_body_is_good), Facebook (facebook.com/amandamartinezbeck), and Twitter (@AmandaMBeck). Conference, retreat, and podcast booking information is available at amandamartinezbeck .com, where you can also find more resources to help you embrace the body God gave you.